Evaluating for Good Practice

Angela Everitt
and
Pauline Hardiker

MACMILLAN

First published 1996 by
MACMILLAN PRESS LTD
Houndmills, Basingstoke, Hampshire RG21 6XS
and London
Companies and representatives
throughout the world

ISBN 0-333-59967-5

A catalogue record for this book is available
from the British Library.

10 9 8 7 6 5 4 3 2 1
05 04 03 02 01 00 99 98 97 96

Printed in Malaysia

Series Standing Order (Practical Social Work)

If you would like to receive future titles in this series as they are published, you can make use of our standing order facility. To place a standing order please contact your bookseller or, in case of difficulty, write to us at the address below with your name and address and the name of the series. Please state with which title you wish to begin your standing order. (If you live outside the UK we may not have the rights for your area, in which case we will forward your order to the publisher concerned.)

Standing Order Service, Macmillan Distribution Ltd,
Houndmills, Basingstoke, Hampshire, RG21 6XS, England.

PRACTICAL SOCIAL WORK

Series Editor: Jo Campling

BASW

Social work is at an important stage in its development. All professions must be responsive to changing social and economic conditions if they are to meet the needs of those they serve. This series focuses on sound practice and the specific contributions which social workers can make to the well-being of our society.

The British Association of Social Workers has always been conscious of its role in setting guidelines for practice and in seeking to raise professional standards. The conception of the Practical Social Work series arose from a survey of BASW members to discover where they, the practitioners in social work, felt there was the most need for new literature. The response was overwhelming and enthusiastic, and the result is a carefully planned, coherent series of books. The emphasis is firmly on practice set in a theoretical framework. The books will inform, stimulate and promote discussion, thus adding to the further development of skills and high professional standards. All the authors are practitioners and teachers of social work representing a wide variety of experience.

A list of publ [illegible] *f*

PRACTICAL SOCIAL WORK

Social Work and Empowerment
Robert Adams

Social Work and Mental Handicap
David Anderson

Beyond Casework
James G. Barber

Social Work with Addictions
James G. Barber

Citizen Involvement
Peter Beresford and Suzy Croft

Practising Social Work Law
Suzy Brave and Michael Preston-Shoot

Social Workers at Risk
Robert Brown, Stanley Bute and Peter Ford

Social Workers and Mental Illness
Alan Butler and Colin Pritchard

Social Work and Europe
Crescy Cannan, Lynn Berry and Karen Lyons

Residential Work
Roger Clough

Social Work and Child Abuse
David M. Cooper and David Ball

Management in Social Work
Veronica Coulshed

Social Work Practice
Veronica Coulshed

Social Work and Local Politics
Paul Daniel and John Wheeler

Sociology in Social Work Practice
Peter R. Day

Anti-Racist Social Work
Lena Dominelli

Working with Abused Children
Delia Doyle

Evaluating for Good Practice
Angela Everitt and Pauline Hardiker

Applied Research for Better Practice
Angela Everitt, Pauline Hardiker, Jane Littlewood and Audrey Mullender

Student Supervision in Social Work
Kathy Ford and Alan Jones

Working with Rural Communities
David Francis and Paul Henderson

Children, their Families and the Law
Michael D.A. Freeman

Family Work with Elderly People
Alison Froggatt

Child Sexual Abuse
Danya Glaser and Stephen Frosh

Computers in Social Work
Bryan Glastonbury

Working with Families
Gill Gorell Barnes

Women, Management and Care
Cordelia Grimwood and Ruth Popplestone

Women and Social Work
Jalna Hanmer and Daphne Statham

Youth Work
Tony Jeffs and Mark Smith (eds)

Problems of Childhood and Adolescence
Michael Kerfoot and Alan Butler

Communication in Social Work
Joyce Lishman

Working with Violence
Carol Lupton and Terry Gillespie (eds)

Social Work with Older People
Mary Marshall and Mary Dixon

Applied Psychology for Social Workers
Paula Nicolson and Rowan Bayne

Crisis Intervention in Social Services
Kieran O'Hagan

Social Work with Disabled People
Michael Oliver

Care Management
Joan Orme and Bryan Glastonbury

Social Care in the Community
Malcolm Payne

Working in Teams
Malcolm Payne

Working with Young Offenders
John Pitts

Effective Groupwork
Michael Preston-Shoot

Effective Probation Practice
Peter Raynor, David Smith and Maurice Vanstone

Social Work with the Dying and Bereaved
Carole R. Smith

Child Care and the Courts
Carole R. Smith, Mary T. Lane and Terry Walsh

Criminology for Social Work
David Smith

Social Work and Housing
Gill Stewart and John Stewart

Focus on Families
Christine Stones

Anti-Discriminatory Practice
Neil Thompson

Dealing with Stress
Neil Thompson, Michael Murphy and Steve Stradling

Working with Mental Illness
Derek Tilbury

Community Work
Alan Twelvetrees

Working with Offenders
Hilary Walker and Bill Beaumont (eds)

Contents

Acknowledgements ix

1 Evaluation in Practice: Our Approach **1**
Taking evaluation seriously 2
Practitioners evaluating 4
Developing a critical approach to evaluation 6
The context 13

2 The Purposes of Evaluation **19**
Evaluation and monitoring 20
Evaluation and research 20
Evaluation and values 23
Evaluation for control 25
Evaluation for 'good' practice 27

3 Facts, Truth and Values **37**
The developing use of evaluation 42
The developing misuse of evaluation 45
Evaluation and the scientific method 46
Values and the scientific method 48
The politics of evaluation 50
Causality and evaluation 51
Evaluating for 'good' practice 53

4 Measuring Performance **57**
Performance measurement and performance indicators 57
Frameworks for measuring performance 59
Measuring performance as a means of control 62
Ways forward in performance measurement 66
Prospects for development 73
There is no going back! 75
Mosaic of indicators 80
In conclusion 82

5	**Towards a Critical Approach to Evaluation**	**83**
	Critical evaluators	84
	Interpretivist evaluations	86
	Formative and summative evaluation	88
	Illuminative evaluation	88
	Actors and stakeholders	89
	Pluralist evaluation	92
	Fourth-generation evaluation	95
	Towards a critical evaluation	98
	The contribution of postmodernist theory to evaluation	105
6	**Designs for Critical Evaluation**	**108**
	A resource map for generating evidence	108
	Analysing discourses	112
7	**Generating Evidence About Practice**	**132**
	Ongoing, serial evaluation	132
	Practice and the practitioner	134
	Understanding methods	137
	Asking users	138
	Well-tried and tested research methods	146
	Dialogical methods	149
	Supervision as an evaluative process	154
8	**Making Judgements and Effecting Change**	**157**
	The need for judgement-making	158
	Interpreting data and evidence	162
	The responsibilities of the evaluator	166
	Values, standards and the notion of the 'good'	170
	Democracy and rights in evaluation	174
9	**Conclusion**	**182**
	Needs	183
	Critical theory	187
	Social work, social welfare and the 'good'	188
	The purpose and focus of critical evaluation	190
	Evaluating for good practice	194

Annotated Bibliography 197
References 203
Author Index 216
Subject Index 218

Acknowledgements

We should like to take this opportunity to thank the managers and officers in the social services and probation departments where our evaluation projects were undertaken. Our thanks also to members of management committees, users, workers and volunteers in voluntary projects and community groups with whom we have engaged in evaluations. To the funders of these evaluations we express our appreciation. Their encouragement and support of our attempts to develop critical approaches to evaluation have been invaluable.

Our ideas for this book have developed in valuable discussions with colleagues, students and practitioners.

In particular, we express our appreciation to Jane Aldgate, Mary Barker, Noel Timms and Andrew Willis. Dorothy Stock Whitaker has taken a lively interest in our work and offered wise advice and guidance. Lucy Panasiuk has once again demonstrated her supurb administrative and word-processing skills with her usual generosity – we thank her.

The evaluation work of the Social Welfare Research Unit owes much to Chris Johnson who, with Tony Jeffs and Pam Carter, helped set up the Unit. As loyal but critical colleagues and friends they continue to be invaluable. And thanks to all colleagues in the Social Welfare Research Unit, research staff, associates and students, for commitment 'beyond the call of duty'.

Jo Campling and Catherine Gray have facilitated our path through to publication.

ANGELA EVERITT
PAULINE HARDIKER

1

Evaluation in Practice: Our Approach

Increasing attention is being paid to evaluation in the personal social services and in social welfare more broadly. The 1980s and 1990s have witnessed new languages and approaches to social welfare. Citizenship, citizen charters and consumerism; inspection and complaints procedures, and quality control requirements of the 1989 Children Act, the 1990 National Health Service and Community Care Act and the Criminal Justice Acts; total quality management; value for money; performance measurement and performance indicators; the need for public services, including voluntary projects, to be publicly accountable for economy, efficiency and effectiveness; all these developments have had the effect of placing evaluation near to the top of the agenda in many social welfare organisations.

We examine critically the place of evaluation in this new political economy of social welfare. We are concerned that, as part of new systems of public sector management, a form of 'managerial evaluation' is developing which, at worst, serves as a mechanism to ensure that practice conforms to New Right policy agendas, and which, at best, will be fudged and regarded with cynicism by practitioners and users alike.

The task we have set ourselves is to retrieve evaluation from being applied as a tool of social control to one that will contribute to the development of 'good' practice. Evaluating for 'good' practice places evaluation firmly within democratic processes involving practitioners and users.

Taking evaluation seriously

It is important that practice is evaluated and that social welfare organisations become evaluative. Policies and practices in social welfare agencies can never be self-justifying. Their aims, activities and consequences may be taken-for-granted, criticised or applauded on a variety of grounds: political, legal, ethical, professional, practical or personal. For example:

- a playscheme run by a voluntary agency may be justified on grounds of its legal mandate, the number of qualified workers it employs or the vested interests of the management committee;
- a child protection service may be justified on the basis of its strategic policy objectives, its case-clearance rates, the proportion of parents prosecuted or the practical activities undertaken;
- a probation programme for high-risk offenders may be applauded because of its open, ethical approach and its engagement with users and their partners;
- programmes for older and disabled people may be criticised because they are deemed to be too costly, to stigmatise users and carers and to intrude too much into people's lives.

There are elements of evaluation in each of these conclusions and judgements like these may be deemed unfair or fair, unjust or just, by different people with diverse interests. A more systematic, explicit and critical evaluative scrutiny needs to take place. Evaluation involves asking and answering questions such as:

- Does it work?
- Does it achieve what was intended?
- Is it worthwhile?
- Is it worth the resources, the money and time spent on it?

- Is it good?
- Is it bad?
- Is it 'good enough'?

These questions demand the generation of evidence about the practice, policy or programme being evaluated. They also necessitate the making of value judgements about that practice, a process made more explicit, accountable and critical if informed with evidence. For example:

- what evidence is used to identify ways in which the number of qualified workers makes a service more effective?
- what evidence is used to show that case-clearance rates provide adequate protection for vulnerable children?
- what evidence is there that an open, ethical approach to users and their partners addresses high-risk offending?
- in what ways are costs related to degrees of risk and vulnerability in programmes for older and disabled people?

This brief excursion into issues of evaluation raises several relevant points:

- judgements about policies and practices are made daily in respect of social welfare;
- these judgements may appear, at first glance, to be quite sophisticated;
- judgements may be positive, negative, implicit or explicit;
- evidence may or may not be used in relation to the abandonment or improvement of programmes;
- different types of evidence are used for different purposes;
- different factors are involved in making judgements about the appropriateness of policies and practices.

In our approach we find it useful to conceptualise evaluation as involving both *the generation of evidence* about an activity, a policy, a programme or a project, and *the process of making judgements about its value.* We pursue an argument to the effect that evidence alone does not add up to the judgement of value, but, at the same time, the process of judgement-making should be informed with evidence.

Practitioners evaluating

We address our writing to practitioners in the broad field of social welfare working in the personal social services, the probation service, and in voluntary sector organisations and projects. Practitioners have always been involved in evaluation: they continually make judgements about the practice of themselves and others. They could not practise otherwise. For example:

- social problems and needs are negotiated with colleagues, users, workers in other agencies, and carers, to work towards sensitive understandings;
- interventions and projects are scrutinised, modified and changed in the light of their relevance to such problems and needs;
- decisions about bringing projects and interventions to conclusion, transfer or renegotiation are made in the light of progress towards achieving objectives.

All of us evaluate all the time in order to take action. Just as we inevitably theorise in practice, think in action, make judgements as to how and when to act, so we also evaluate in practice. We make judgements as to whether something is worth doing, whether the programme or policy is working well, whether our colleague, boss or the next-door team is competent. We are sometimes pleased with what we've managed to achieve, sometimes less so, perhaps having niggling doubts or even substantial worries. We may feel passion and commitment to the project in which we are working. We may feel jaded and a little disgruntled that the project has lost its way. We may find ourselves in open disagreement with others in the organisation about what is being undertaken and with what effects, and decide to try to bring about change or leave.

Judgements may take many forms and practitioners usually evaluate in relatively implicit ways:

- she seems to be thriving
- Mrs X seems less stressed
- his speech has improved dramatically
- she has settled in well
- Mrs Y has started a part-time job and the family are planning their first holiday.

These evaluations are often perfectly sound. But evaluations also may be of a self-justifying or rhetorical nature, or they may be of a spurious scientific kind, as when practices are both described numerically and considered out of context. Discharge rates, for example, may be used to measure success whereas, if understood within policy and procedural contexts, they might reveal evidence, not of success, but of bed-clearing operations or amnesties.

We may decide to examine our practice more thoroughly and systematically than leaving it to our subjective, and often implicit, feelings. We may decide to become more aware of these feelings, to try to understand them in terms of where they have come from, how they have arisen, upon what evidence are they based, and can they be justified.

We may go further in evaluating our work. We may decide to ask other people what they think about what we're doing: colleagues, users, workers in other agencies, councillors, potential users and/or community activists. We may decide to set up an evaluation employing external consultants to undertake the work or assist us in the process.

Alternatively, others, such as managers, councillors, external funders, may decide that our work or our project be evaluated. It is these approaches to evaluation, through specially designed evaluation studies or through other organisational evaluative systems, that are the subject of this book. We are concerned with evaluation that is systematic, explicit and involves independent and critical judgement-making about the value of practice. And we are wanting to develop an approach to evaluation that sits comfortably, but critically, within the repertoire of the practitioner. In the end, our interest in evaluation is a commitment to the development of 'good' practice. This is what we demand of evaluation and evaluative systems: that they contribute to practice developing in the direction of the 'good'.

Developing a critical approach to evaluation

In the chapter which follows this introduction, we draw up a set of conditions for an approach to evaluation that would promote 'good' or 'good enough' practice and inhibit 'poor' practice or even 'corrupt' practice. These conditions include:

- recognising the importance of collective debate, dialogue and openness;
- being sceptical of rational-technical ways of knowing;
- recognising power, powerlessness and empowerment in being a knower or being treated as 'other';
- genuine dialogue between users and practitioners and between those within the organisation;
- attending to purpose, including values, rather than only products in the form of outputs.

We appraise different approaches to evaluation for their ability to meet these conditions. We consider ways of evaluating that are underpinned by the traditional scientific method, what we call 'rational-technical' approaches, and ways that rely upon subjective experiences, 'interpretivist' approaches. We find both of these wanting and draw upon critical and postmodernist theories of knowledge and power in order to develop an approach to evaluation that is critical and potentially more able to facilitate informed and open debate about the value of practices, policies and programmes in social welfare.

Our argument for an approach to evaluation for 'good' practice is developed as follows:

- We start in this introductory chapter by placing evaluation in the context of the new political economy of social welfare and in the context of practitioner ways of working.
- In Chapter 2, we distinguish evaluation from monitoring and from research. We reflect on the multiple reasons why organisations and projects engage in evaluation. We propose that, if evaluation is to facilitate 'good' practice, then it must be undertaken in ways that strengthen the conditions that prevent practice becoming corrupt.
- The debate about knowledge as facts, truth or values, which informs different approaches to evaluation, is presented in Chapter 3. In particular, we reflect upon ways in which evaluation adopts causal rational-technical models of knowing, and the implications of this. This is particularly pertinent in the 1990s when such an approach to evaluation has become so prevalent in public sector management in statutory and voluntary sectors.
- The rational-technical approach to evaluation is most clearly, and increasingly routinely, articulated in performance measurement using performance indicators. This is considered in detail in Chapter 4. While we find this rational-technical approach wanting in terms

of its ability to meet the conditions for evaluating for 'good' practice, at the same time we explore ways in which the measuring of performance may be helpful in generating evidence of the effectiveness of practice, policies and programmes in meeting their declared objectives.

- Different approaches to ways in which we understand or explain aspects of the social world give rise to different evaluation models. These models are traced developmentally and presented in Chapter 5. We conclude that chapter by drawing upon critical and postmodernist theories of knowledge in order to develop a critical approach to evaluation.
- In Chapter 6, having reached a critical approach to evaluation, we develop a methodology for such evaluation. We apply this to evaluating policies and practices within the 1989 Children Act, 1990 National Health Service and Community Care Act and within the Probation Service.
- Our critical approach to evaluation distinguishes between generating evidence of the policy, practice or programme being evaluated and making judgements about it informed by this evidence. In Chapter 7, we suggest ways in which evidence of practice may be generated. In doing so, we do not attempt to replicate research methods texts but focus more upon other ways of generating data that we have found useful in our own evaluation practice. Our approach to generating evidence of practice is one that values both data that can be analysed quantitatively and qualitatively. In other words, both numbers and stories can be valuable in building up evidence of practice.
- Pursuing the conceptual distinction between generating evidence of the practice and making judgements about its value, in Chapter 8 we look at the process of judgement-making. Within a rational-technical approach to evaluation the relationship between

evaluation and change is often treated as linear with the product of evaluation (its findings) fed into the policy-making arena. Within our critical approach, we regard the relationship between generating evidence and making judgements of value as dynamic, one is integral to the other. The emphasis in evaluation moves from product to process. In this chapter, we attempt to provide a flavour of this by reflecting upon the relationship between the process of making judgements about the value of practice and the process of change in the direction of the 'good'.

- Our conclusions lead us back to reflecting upon the conditions we set for an approach to evaluation that would promote 'good' practice and inhibit 'poor' practice. We invite the reader to do the same.
- We illustrate our argument throughout with examples of evaluations, mainly drawn from our own evaluation practice and that of colleagues with whom we work.

Here we provide two examples which illustrate the ways in which our approach moves us from rational-technical and interpretivist approaches to evaluation to one that is critical.

Case example

So-called 'objective' data have been produced regarding the reduction in Care Orders and measures such as Emergency Protection Orders during the first year's implementation of the 1989 Children Act. Does a reduction in compulsory orders mean that the new legislation is being implemented effectively?

The 'facts' may be understood in a variety of ways leading to quite different evaluative judgements about the effectiveness of the new legislation.

- Adopting a rational-technical model of evaluation, court

orders may be treated as outputs of services. Numerical data demonstrating a decrease in these orders may lead to an evaluative judgement of good practice in terms of the effectiveness of the 'non-interventionist' principle embodied in the Children Act.

- Employing an 'interpretivist' evaluation approach, the subjective experiences of those involved in the process may be treated as data. Lawyers may talk of the effectiveness of the Act, approving of the apparent reduction in care orders. Social workers may express more ambivalence because in their experience the more precise requirements for evidence for care orders are accompanied by difficulties in providing adequate protection for vulnerable children. Children and their parents may feel they have been put through hurdles, or made to feel deviant through the ways 'significant harm' is interpreted. At the same time, they may experience freedom from state controls through the 'no order' thresholds requirements.
- A critical approach to evaluation explores the structures and processes through which output data and descriptions of diverse subjective experiences are produced. This will be illustrated briefly at this point and systematically throughout the book:

  – The first question to be asked about output data is whether the inputs and throughputs have changed and affected outcomes. If the circumstances and characteristics of children entering the system have changed, different outputs might be expected. Fewer care orders might be made because of variations in the age, gender, ethnicity, socio-economic status of children and parenting/family patterns. The input/output model can be criticised in its own terms as a model and from a critical perspective. If the input is the same, the throughput may have changed. Social workers may be using more preventive family support services, community development or task-centred approaches to child protection that obviate the need for compulsory orders. Alternatively, social work practices may have stayed the same. The reduction in care orders may result from the new requirements for evidence making it difficult to establish the threshold criteria needed before they are made, leaving children without adequate protection. Whatever the input, throughput and output processes, what are the longer-term outcomes for children and their families involved in these situations? Which children and which families? Is their physical, psychological and social functioning better, the same, or worse because an Order has or has not been made? Is this the same for children and families irrespective of social class and ethnicity?

– The subjective experiences of different parties in the process have also to be interrogated. It is one thing to document the richness and variety of these experiences: their underlying structures and processes also need to be analysed. There is unlikely to be a straightforward connection between client satisfaction and the result of court proceedings. Some parents may be relieved when a court order is made, others may feel let-down. Whatever the outcome, many will judge the processes by which it is achieved. Did they feel they were listened to, were they helped, were adequate explanations provided, etc? Given the complexities of care proceedings, it is to be expected that different parties will have different views about them. Subjective experiences have to be analysed in relation to their situations and the stakes they hold in the matter. Even when their interests diverge, it is important to know whether everyone was listened to and their views represented, irrespective of their social class or ethnicity, of whether they are children or adults, lone parents or lesbian mothers.

From a critical perspective, evaluation involves processes of dialogue and practice and policy change. The structures and processes through which apparently objective facts and subjective experiences are generated and filtered need to be interrogated. Furthermore, the purpose of evaluation is not merely to provide better or more realistic accounts of phenomena, but to place a value on them and to change situations, practices and people's circumstances accordingly.

Our second illustrative example is drawn from practice within the Community Care legislation.

Case example

Initial data on the implementation of the 1990 National Health Service and Community Care Act indicate that the legislation is being implemented 'effectively' because the number of people placed in independent residential and nursing homes has fallen and the number of places available in local authority residences has decreased. The other side of this coin is that local authorities are under-spending their community care budgets. The subjective experiences of many participants involved in the new arrangements indicate that:

– users and carers think they have few or fewer choices;
– social workers think they are being required to practise accountancy;
– managers are being held accountable for budgets;
– some private entrepreneurs feel angry because of business opportunities lost;
– legislators think they are achieving their aims in reducing the perverse incentive to choose residential instead of domiciliary options;
– the private domiciliary market is developing very slowly.

Again, these are preliminary and relatively superficial observations, even evaluations, on the implementation of new legislation. It is necessary to go beyond such numerical evidence and subjective experiences because such data reflect only the tip of the iceberg of complex structures and processes which constitute the new community care arrangements. Practice must be contextualised. The arrangements of practice must be evaluated.

We opened this introductory chapter by referring to the new language and approaches of the political economy of social welfare in the 1990s. For us, a strong motive for writing this book has been the growing significance of evaluation within new forms of management in the public sector. It is to this that we now return in the concluding section of this introduction. We focus upon selected issues of this restructuring in order to locate demands for evaluation in the context of political economy. These will then be used as a springboard to identify the prospects for evaluating for 'good' practice. In our view, we need to begin to think differently about the purposes of evaluation and to develop new approaches to address these purposes.

The context

The restructuring of the Welfare State has been a very complex political, economic and social process. Historically bound and shaped, it has been driven ideologically by Thatcherism. The democratic consensus about the Welfare State which lasted for about thirty years, a short time in historical terms, was founded upon the Keynes–Beveridge equation. Government had an economic role to manage demand in the market economy and a social role to insure against the hazards of this economy. This equation legitimated large-scale state interventions in economic and social spheres.

This consensus and legitimation was challenged in the 1970s in all advanced industrialised societies, fanned by the decline in economic growth, the rise in unemployment and the hiatus between revenue and expenditure plans (Hoyes *et al.*, 1992; Jackson, 1988a; 1988b; Jackson and Palmer,

1992; Taylor-Gooby and Lawson, 1993; George and Miller, 1994). The monetarism and managerialism of the New Right brought with it the need for fiscal containment, the search for value for money, the ideology of rolling back the frontiers of the state and the desire to improve public sector management. Each meant in turn the need for more information about performance in the public sector (Jackson, 1988a). Approaches thus had to be developed to evaluating practices in social welfare and penal agencies.

The political requirements included a belief in the need to restore public confidence in government, to increase accountability, to improve managerial competence and to control public expenditure (Carter, 1991). The New Right was crystal clear in its critique of the Welfare State which was said to slow down economic growth and wealth creation and to undermine entrepreneurial effort and work incentives. A parallel critique of the Welfare State was provided by welfare pluralists who challenged large-scale monopolistic state bureaucracies and outlined alternative decentralised pluralistic service structures based on user participation (Hadley and Hatch, 1981).

Even in its heyday, the Welfare State had not been left to develop in uncontrolled ways. The problem of the absence of a national strategy for planning and resource allocation alongside lack of appropriate structures underlay the reform efforts of the Heath government in the early 1970s (Gray and Jenkins, 1993). These included corporate management in local authorities and planning and resource management systems in the NHS. New mechanisms were set up for Programme Analysis and Review. The Cabinet 'think tank', the Central Policy Review Staff, also continued these developments. However, by the early 1980s, these developments had foundered.

> The reason for these failures of rational planning, policy evaluation and policy analysis are often peculiar to individual cases.

> However, there are also common strands, not least that many reform efforts failed to meet technical, organisational and political preconditions essential for their survival. (Gray and Jenkins, 1993: 11)

The information technology was not in place to meet the technical requirements; the large-scale, 'rudderless', monopolistic nature of many state bureaucracies could not be controlled as 'rationally' as intended; the new forms of control were in direct conflict with many political communities such as local democracies, committees and user groups. Rational-technical modes did not fit with democratic processes, an important point which underpins our argument in this book for an approach to evaluation that is critical and democratic.

One of the next developments was New Public Management. This emphasised

> fostering a managerial environment which is attentive to performance when funds are parcelled out (Schick, 1990: 26),

wherein spenders are turned into managers and a tighter relationship is forged between resources and results, achieved partly by decentralising structures so that managers can be held accountable for what they do and spend. Other developments included various sympathetic 'think tanks', for example the Institute for Economic Affairs, the launch of efficiency scrutinies, and the development of Management Information Systems. The Financial Management Initiative (FMI) was introduced to promote accountable management through management information systems, decentralised budgets and performances appraised. This became the model for similar initiatives in police, probation, education and social services departments although a variety of approaches were tried out.

> For some it is first and foremost a system for controlling

> costs, for others, a more comprehensive system for planning, allocating and controlling resources, while for a few it is a more general philosophy and regime of management. (Gray *et al.*, 1991: 49)

Sometimes these multiple objectives came into conflict with each other: there were many reasons why they were difficult to operationalise. It was unclear whether or not the new measures represented improved monitoring systems. Are outputs intermediate or final measures? Are there any credible measures of efficiency and effectiveness? Are the measures actually used? (Carter, 1988a)

The Audit Commission (1991) spearheaded many initiatives through producing annual local authority profiles, special studies of particular services [such as housing and community care] and key indicators (for example, for home care services). It recommended the development in local authorities of business plans, management and performance assessment systems. The strengthened Social Services Inspectorate also initiated key indicators for use by local authorities. These included financial data, social needs, staffing, expenditure and services for different user groups (Department of Health, 1994).

The new public sector management and the ideology of the New Right has had enormous implications for the structure and functions of local authorities. Gray and Jenkins (1993) even ask if there is anything substantive left of a provider model of local government. The key features of these changes are set out below and are now familiar to those practising within the Community Care legislation and the 1989 Children Act. The place of evaluation within them is significant.

- the enabling authority;
- division between commissioner and provider roles;
- using and stimulating the mixed economy of welfare;
- compulsory competitive tendering;

- arm's-length inspection units;
- complaints procedures;
- the slow but inexorable development of 'quasi-markets' and devolved budgeting;
- the ideology of consumerism, including user empowerment.

We have argued in this chapter that evaluation is important to guard against self-justifying practices, to make judgements about the value of practice explicit, open and accountable, and to inform judgements with evidence. We have suggested that evaluation may be key to the development of 'good' practice and to the inhibition of 'poor' or even 'corrupt' practice. For us, then, it is important that evaluation is not co-opted by New Right approaches to public sector management.

The political thrust underlying developments in the public services and the Welfare State has been to break up what were seen as monopolistic, large-scale state bureaucracies shielded from competition. Market mechanisms have been introduced supposedly to increase efficiency, economy, effectiveness and accountability. The role of local government in social policy and provision through local democratic processes has been reduced. And underlying all these developments is a deprofessionalising tendency, especially in relation to the semi-professions.

In contrast, retrieving evaluation for 'good' practice will entail developing approaches to the making of informed judgements about the value of practice in social welfare that enhance the possibility of practice working in the direction of the 'good': working towards justice, equality and human well-being. It follows that a necessary requirement of evaluation is that it is firmly placed within democratic processes: that all with an interest in the social welfare practice have opportunity to judge its value taking account of the fact that, because of gender, race, age, class, economic status, sexual orientation and disability, people are not in equal positions to do this. And finally, evaluation becomes an essential ingredient in the repertoire of the practitioner. As such, professionalism in social welfare practice is reclaimed in the sense of the practitioner taking responsibility for ensuring 'good' practice.

2

The Purposes of Evaluation

In the introductory chapter we revealed the context of the changing political economy of social welfare in which evaluation has become a significant managerialist strategy for efficiency and control. As House remarks about Britain in his appraisal of evaluation in advanced capitalist societies:

> The government has tried to install a culture of management modelled on the corporate sector in order to curtail the spending of local governments and the demands of professionals and unions. Professional authority is subsumed under managerial authority. Managerial evaluation, focused on efficiency and productivity under direct government control, has been attempted in many departments. (House, 1993: x)

The purpose of evaluation in this context is to do with ensuring the efficiency, economy, effectiveness and accountability of organisations and projects operating in the market place outside of processes of democratic control and professional standards. In this chapter, in order to resist the co-option of evaluation in this context, we go back to square one to reflect on the purposes of evaluation. Why evaluate? We start by distinguishing evaluation from monitoring and from research.

Evaluation and monitoring

Evaluation is related to monitoring, but it is also different and distinct. Monitoring is the process of keeping track of what is happening, watching what is happening and documenting this in some way. When a policy is decided upon and implemented, it may be agreed in the organisation to watch what happens. In implementing equal opportunities policies in the recruitment and selection of staff, for example, monitoring mechanisms may be set up to watch what happens in terms of: who applies for jobs with the organisation and who is successful in getting employment, taking account of their sex, sexual orientation, ethnicity, age, and whether they are disabled or not. Similarly, monitoring the users of projects and organisations can serve to keep track of whether the services are accessible to all people in the community.

Such data created through monitoring processes can be valuable to inform and facilitate the evaluation of practice. Knowing what happens in recruitment and selection, for example, helps to make informed judgements about the value of the equal opportunities recruitment and selection policy. Knowing that some members of the local population systematically do not use the services of the organisation helps inform the judgement about the appropriateness of the services, and/or the ways in which they are offered and made accessible to all irrespective of gender, age, race, class, economic status, sexual orientation and disability.

Evaluation and research

Evaluation is also related to research in terms of getting to know about the practice being evaluated, generating the evidence of that practice. This process of getting to know may be built into the organisation through monitoring systems and through other systems of documenting practice. Provided that attention is given to the reliability and validity of information collected routinely, evaluation may draw on such information as data. In Chapter 7, we consider in more detail ways in which data may be generated for evaluation.

It may be, though, that in addition to ongoing, built-in recording and monitoring systems, or as a substitute for them, the evaluation has to start with getting to know about what is going on. The process of getting to know is one of being 'research-minded' (Everitt *et al.*, 1992). It is a process of finding out about the practice, documenting it, scrutinising it for its assumptions and implications. It is a process that has no limits both in terms of questions that may be asked of practice and in terms of the possibility of the ongoing and never-ending nature of questioning.

So getting to know about practice in order to make judgements about its value involves researching that practice:

- What is the policy? How, and in what ways, is it implemented? By whom? What resources does it depend upon? What are the effects of implementing the policy? What does it achieve? Who benefits? Who loses? What unintended consequences occur? How does it affect other policies and organisations?
- What is the activity? What happens? Who is involved in it? What do they do? With whom and for whom is this activity undertaken? What resources does it take up? What other activities does it depend on? How does it relate to policy? What effects does it have? Are there measurable outcomes?
- What is the project all about? What does it do? Who is involved in the project? What resources are going into the project? How does it relate to other organisations? How is it managed? How is it evaluated? How does it ensure good practice? What issues are raised through the course of its work? How are these issues addressed?

Case example

A voluntary community education project, active in a particular locality for ten years, decided to undertake an evaluation. The management committee and workers of the project met with the evaluators to agree the design and scope of the evaluation. One of the first things they did was to agree on the questions that would be put to the project in order to document it and subject it to critical scrutiny:

- Who uses the project and who doesn't, and why, taking account of gender, ethnicity, disability, and age?
- How is the project seen in the area by local people and agencies?
- What are the project's main areas of work and how have these developed historically?
- Have these areas of work been developed through the implementation of a successful strategy and to what extent have they been influenced by external factors?
- How much is the project's present pattern of work determined by the availability of funding and the changing funding patterns for further and adult education and leisure and community services?
- How has the project's commitment to local management been maintained at a time of increasing complexity and what additional support and training does the management committee require?
- Are there aims that have not yet been fully met and why?
- What is the range of community education and training activities in the city, and in the particular locality, and what are the relationships between these activities?
- How does the project fit in with the wider network of organisations in the city?
- How has the project changed and developed over the last ten years and who's gained and who's lost from these changes?
- What ideas of education and training do people have both in the local community and external agencies, including funders? (Everitt and Green, 1995)

These questions were to be asked of this community education project in the course of the evaluation. Answers would be sought from people connected with the project and from other sources such as case files, committee minutes, records, diaries etc. Through this process, data will be generated to answer the questions and an analysis of the data made to make meaning of them. These stages in the evaluation process are those of any piece of research. There is an increasing wealth of literature available for practitioners wanting to learn more about the process of doing research (see, for example, Whitaker and Archer, 1989; Whitaker, 1992; Everitt *et al.*, 1992; and Everitt and Gibson, 1994, which contains an annotated bibliography of accessible research methods texts reproduced before the bibliography at the end of this book).

Evaluation and values

The questions addressed to the community education project within the evaluation study raise other issues. First, the questions are not plucked out of thin air. It is not a random list of questions. They relate to the project and to what people connected to the project think should be asked of it. The questions are theoretically informed. They are informed with theories as to what the project should be doing and might not be, what it should be achieving and might not be, factors that might have enhanced the project in achieving its objectives, and those that might have distracted the project from its purpose. They are also questions that have been prioritised. Other questions may well have been asked. Thus, they are theoretically informed to explore issues that the project may have encountered in pursuing its purpose.

Second, the questions were raised by people related to the project in different ways: the workers, members of the voluntary management committee, and external evaluators.

Thinking about who should be responsible for, and involved in, evaluation will be explored in more detail below.

Third, not only are the questions theoretically informed with notions of the purpose of the project, its effectiveness, and constraints and opportunities it has encountered, but they also contain within them notions of the 'good'. Implied within the first question, 'who uses the project and who doesn't, and why, taking account of gender, ethnicity, disability, and age?', is the notion that the project would be engaging in 'good' practice if it were used by all sections of the community irrespective of sex, ethnicity, disability, and age. From the example of the community education project, we can see that having a notion of the 'good' informs the evaluation design: it suggests the questions to be asked in getting to know about the practice that is being evaluated, and it helps decide who should be involved in setting the questions.

Evaluation, as the term implies, is imbued with values. Values and notions of the 'good' are significant throughout the evaluation process, from its inception, implementation through to feedback and dissemination. Having a notion of the 'good' crucially comes into play in moving from research to evaluation, from having to get to know about the practice to making judgements about its worth.

The questions to be answered through evaluation, and it is these that distinguish evaluation from research and from monitoring, are:

- Now that we know what's happening, what value do we place on it?
- Is the practice 'good' given the resources that have been put into it and the opportunities that it has had?
- Is the practice 'good enough' given the constraints upon it, the difficulties it's encountered, the limited resources it has had devoted to it?
- Is the practice not good enough and do therefore changes need to be made if it is to continue?

Evaluation involves making judgements about the 'good'. It is a value-laden and political process and an important part of the repertoire of the professional practitioner. This is our contention. Not everyone will agree with our approach to evaluation and it is therefore important that we provide more argument for what we contend. This is the purpose of this chapter.

Evaluation for control

Social welfare organisations, voluntary projects, community groups and practitioners will commission and/or engage in evaluation for a range of reasons. Often voluntary projects are prompted into having an evaluation done because of the requirement to demonstrate their value to funders, either as a condition of that funding, or in the attempt to secure funding in the next round. Providing evidence of effectiveness may be one of the conditions of funding or indeed may be written into the contract made between the purchasing authority and the provider. Statutory authorities, too, health authorities, local authorities, schools and colleges, for example, have to demonstrate the ways in which resources have been used and with what effects.

Social welfare practitioners and organisations not only have a responsibility to evaluate themselves, but also to evaluate the contexts and policy frameworks within which they operate. There are two aspects to this.

First, to evaluate practice without taking account of the context of that practice, and the policies which constrain it or provide opportunities for it, is to take a very blinkered approach. De-contextualising practice in such a way assumes that practice exists as a commodity on its own that may be separated out for study. It is an atheoretical approach which serves to de-politicise practice. Practice is constructed within legislative, policy and funding processes and is shaped through dimensions of class, gender, race, age, sexuality and disability. The ways in which practice is talked about, and communicated, by those involved in it – users, workers, funders, managers, policymakers – differ. All of these different processes contribute to the ever-changing, and contested, constructions of what practice is. To assume that it is something outside of these processes usually means accepting taken-for-granted ways of understanding the practice. The political relationship between taken-for-granted understandings and the dominant and prevalent ways of seeing things in a society divided by gender, race, class, sexuality, disability and age should make us extremely wary of evaluations that focus only on the practice as though it exists uncontentiously within a policy and social vacuum.

The second aspect of de-contextualising evaluation is that such an evaluative process removes policy and social structures and processes from critical scrutiny. Through their work, social welfare organisations develop, or could be encouraged to develop, understandings of the effects of social and economic policies and of the practices of organisations on people's lives. Those committed to social welfare have an important role to play in making known such effects and their impact on continuing and increasing disadvantage and inequality.

De-contextualised evaluation that scrutinises practice as commodity not only fails to provide opportunities for learning of the effects of discriminatory social and economic policies and processes, but also may do just the opposite and serve to support these processes. 'Managerial evaluation', with its emphasis on demonstration of outcomes and its connection with decisions about continuing funding, encourages organisations and projects to report success, to indicate that intended outcomes have been achieved.

Failure, on the contrary, might be expected in many cases in social welfare. It would not be surprising to find, through evaluations, that social welfare programmes have not been successful, or as successful as intended, given minimal funding and resources in the context of massive social and economic problems. Such evaluations could be valuable in learning about people's lives and the state of community projects, at times of long-term unemployment in desolate and crime-ridden inner-city areas. They could help build a picture that would be useful to inform political and policy dialogue. They would most probably also bring about an end to the programme or project being evaluated. The decision to discontinue with funding would be made on supposedly rational grounds informed by an evaluation that reported failure rather than successful achievement of measurable outcomes. The cut in budget would certainly be legitimated by reference to rational decision-making informed by evaluation.

> As economies falter and governments lose legitimacy, evaluation has been a tool for informing and legitimising the actions that governments must take, particularly budget cutting. (House, 1993: xi)

So we find that the purpose of evaluation might be to demonstrate success at a time of acute social and economic failure. Evaluations should therefore also endeavour to identify any structural forces underlying possible programme failures.

Evaluation for 'good' practice

The purpose of evaluation in social welfare should be to promote 'good' practice. Such evaluations would take account of the social, economic and policy contexts within which the organisation operates and through which social problems and personal troubles develop. Evaluation may take on board both aspects of the context as we illustrated above. It may conceptualise the meanings of practice as constructed through social processes and language and have as its purpose the deconstruction of these meanings. The intention of such an evaluation would be twofold: to expose powerful processes through which some people and groups benefit and others lose out, and to provide opportunity for alternative meanings to be articulated.

Case example

An arts and disability voluntary organisation established a project with the social services department of the local authority to place arts workers in elderly persons' homes in the borough. External evaluators were commissioned to undertake an evaluation to ascertain the extent to which the arts in the homes enhanced the quality of the lives of the older residents. One way to have designed the evaluation would have been to ascertain the objectives of the arts work and, using criteria, measure the extent to which these had been achieved. The evaluator, though, spent some time conceptualising the practice. By asking about the practice, talking with the workers, the arts workers, the care assistants, the homes managers, and the older residents themselves, the evaluator was able to generate data that illustrated different meanings of arts in older people's homes.

- Some saw art as activity implying: production and productivity; the requirement of skills and competence; the recognition of expertise; and being external to the inner selves of participants.
- Some saw art as therapy implying: treatment; applied by one, the worker on the other, the resident; inequality between therapist and client; the production of change and correcting deficiency.
- Some saw art as a means of promoting conversation implying: communication; recognition of self and other; reciprocity and equality; mutual learning and reflection. (Everitt, 1994)

This teasing out of the meanings of the practice provided a framework through which the practice could be understood, analysed, communicated and debated. The different meanings of the arts project interacted to a lesser or greater extent with other processes operating in the homes. Arts as therapy and activity served to enhance those prevailing processes that objectified the older residents. Arts as conversation provided opportunity for those involved in the project, workers and residents, who were keen to work towards empowerment.

Evaluating the social, economic and policy contexts within which practice develops and social problems and personal ills are generated is an important purpose of evaluation for 'good' practice. Social welfare organisations and projects have a valuable role to play in reporting on the ills of society: on the intended and unintended consequences of social and economic policies and their effect on society moving towards equality, justice and well-being (Mills, 1959). Social work and social administration have important, although somewhat neglected, histories in this respect (see Everitt *et al.*, 1992). Sociologists have criticised their peers for not being committed enough to using their craft as a 'civilising' influence upon government (Nicolaus, 1973; Townsend, 1981). Townsend points out the dangers of sociologists acquiescing with 'conventional definitions and assessments of the achievements of social policy' (Townsend, 1981: 30) in both their contemporary and historical analyses of social policy. He calls upon sociologists, and we would address this to evaluators,

> to build public confidence in their capacities to specify what are the short-term and long-term social effects of government policies; explain the existence and severity of acknowledged social problems; call attention to hitherto unacknowledged social problems; show how the body of information (including official statistics) used as a basis for social action can be made more complete as well as relevant, and begin to construct

more coherent and appropriate alternative social policies. (Townsend, 1981: 33)

As well as scrutinising the context within organisations and projects, perhaps within teams or residential establishments, management and/or staff may decide to evaluate their work, or have their work evaluated, so that they are better informed about how effectively they are meeting needs and fulfilling their objectives. It may be that a new policy is now being implemented and there is interest in evaluating its effectiveness. It may be that those involved in an innovatory programme of work are keen to learn from it. Perhaps the staff group is planning to review its operations and feels that it would be better able to do this with some analysis of its effectiveness to date.

Another common reason to evaluate is to make the work of the organisation more visible to its members, its funders, its users and potential users, and to other organisations. This may well be related to the process of negotiating funding through grant applications or contracting. It also may be that members of the organisation, workers, managers, members of the management committee or councillors, feel that the organisation, or a particular project within it, has something to tell the world. Perhaps they think that new ground is being broken or that the experiences, including difficulties, of the organisation should be shared more broadly.

Sometimes it is decided to evaluate the practice because difficulties have arisen. These may be related to cuts in resources or to increased responsibilities having been imposed with new legislation. The difficulties may be associated with increasing lack of agreement within the team or project as to priorities and appropriate working practices. It may be that the management committee has become worn out and problems are being experienced in attracting new members.

The purpose of evaluation that underpins all these different motives and reasons is to scrutinise services and practices in such a way as to ensure 'good' practice. This may not be uppermost in people's minds or on the agenda of the organisations concerned. They may well engage in evaluation just because they have to or because there is no other way to get resourced in the future. And just as research may be commissioned to delay or subvert an impending policy change or as a challenge to existing power relations and practices, so evaluation may be undertaken with the same motives. Nevertheless, implicit within each of the reasons is engagement in a process concerned with demonstrating 'good' practice or exposing practice which is not so good.

In social work, our attention has been drawn to the need to develop approaches to evaluation that will not only ensure 'good' practice, but will detect and make visible practice that is not so good or even is corrupt and abusive. Wardhaugh and Wilding (1993), reflecting on corruptions in care, draw distinctions between that form of bad practice which is as a result of 'a passive neglect of the principles of good practice' (Wardhaugh and Wilding, 1993: 5) and that which amounts to 'an active betrayal of the basic values on which the organisation is supposedly based' (Wardhaugh and Wilding, 1993: 5). Furthermore, they distinguish between corrupt practice which is implemented to meet the policy goals of the organisation and may be, as in the case of Pindown (Levy and Kahan, 1991), professionally articulated and corrupt practice which is contrary to professional and organisational goals, such as sexual abuse in children's homes (Craft, 1993; Kirkwood, 1993).

Wardhaugh and Wilding usefully propose a number of conditions which give rise to, and allow for, the weakening of 'the normal canons of good practice in the human services' (Wardhaugh and Wilding, 1993: 6). We have taken these conditions and, turning them around, propose them as conditions that need to be met by an approach to evaluation for which the practitioner takes responsibility and through which the practitioner may work to ensure 'good' practice'.

- Corruption of care depends on the neutralisation of normal moral concerns. Clients come to be seen as 'less than human' and 'other'. Being bureaucratic, rule following and procedural, has the effect of 'silencing moral considerations' and 'seeks to adjust human actions to an ideal of rationality' (Wardhaugh and Wilding, 1993: 7).

  Evaluation for 'good' practice depends upon outlets for moral debate. Care needs to be taken not to develop rational-technical approaches, not to objectify clients and not to dichotomise workers and clients in the evaluation relationship.
- Corruption of care is closely connected with the balance of power and powerlessness in organisations. Power and powerlessness corrupt and both clients and workers may become taken-for-granted, seldom consulted and reduced as 'full moral beings' (Wardhaugh and Wilding, 1993: 12). Dimensions of gender and race relate to the powerlessness of clients and workers.

  Evaluation for 'good' practice must take account of power and powerlessness, of race and gender, disability and social class, and create in clients and workers feelings that they matter and that their commitment to the project and to its achieving high standards is important.
- Corruption of care is associated with particular pressures and kinds of work. In some situations, the gap between what happens in practice and official policy value statements and intentions is such that the latter lose any legitimacy. And 'where work is difficult, and resources are short, the emphasis is on survival, on getting by' (Wardhaugh and Wilding, 1993: 15).

  Evaluation for 'good' practice must provide a means through which users are able to engage in dialogue with the organisation, rather than only be on the receiving end of mission and customer care statements. It must also provide a means through which practitioners may engage in dialogue within the organisation about decreasing resources and pressures of work.

- Corruption of care is underpinned by management failure. The organisation loses sense of its purpose in terms of 'the basic humanity and rights of service users and. . . . ideas of good practice' (Wardhaugh and Wilding, 1993: 18). Means, or secondary objectives, take over as aims. The smooth-running of the organisation, consensus and productivity within the organisation become goals. Lay management systems operate in ways that are too timid and controlled by professionals.

  Evaluation for 'good' practice requires that purposes are debated and acknowledged. Technically achievable and measurable objectives should not take the place of fundamental purposes. Debating differences in views about good practice becomes essential in the organisation even if this means hosting conflictual discussions. Some people, for example professionals and experts in the organisation, should not be regarded as having any greater say than others when it comes to judging good practice.

- Corruption of care is more likely in closed, inward-looking organisations. Group loyalty, the bureaucratic dodging and side-stepping of complaints and criticisms, the dampening of the possibility of awkward questions being raised – all are features of 'the enclosed organisation (which) develops and maintains a pattern of practice which is routinised and conservative. It expects little of staff and clients. Its aspirations are low – control, order and the absence of trouble' (Wardaugh and Wilding, 1993: 22).

Evaluation for 'good' practice depends upon complaints and criticisms being a feature of the organisation, encouraged and taken seriously. Questioning of policies and practices should be the order of the day. Practices should be constantly and continuously scrutinised with the question 'why are we working in this way?' rather than assuming that because that has been the way of working, then so be it.

- Corruption of care goes along with the lack of clear lines and mechanisms of accountability. Users, and their families and friends, and local people, have no recognised and authoritative involvement in the organisation so 'everything depends on the quality, commitment and values of the front-line staff' (Wardaugh and Wilding, 1993: 25).

Evaluation for 'good' practice involves recognised and meaningful principles of public accountability. People outside the organisation, as users, potential users, relatives, friends and local people are regarded as having an essential role to play in evaluation.

- Corruption of care is supported through particular models of work and organisation, such as 'faith in self-sustaining power of the professional ethic' coupled with hierarchical structures which provide for little legitimacy to be accorded to workers' views (Wardaugh and Wilding, 1993: 26).

Evaluation for 'good' practice depends on organisations being open to debate and to the views of people at all levels, particularly those working directly in the delivery of services. Legitimacy of informed opinion and seniority, power and status are not equated.

- Corruption of care is fostered with certain client groups. Treatment with risk of abuse may develop with clients defined as 'less than persons' (Wardhaugh and Wilding, 1993: 27) and those that generate few rewards for care staff and have little respect and regard paid to them by their families and society generally.

Evaluation for 'good' practice must develop ways of involving those who otherwise, through incapacity or disability, through violence or alienation, may be excluded or may exclude themselves from forums within the organisation which serve to bring workers and clients together on equal terms.

We may now summarise a number of principles which any evaluation system should adopt to ensure 'good' practice:

- the importance of moral debate and everybody, irrespective of power, status and position, having the right to legitimate opinions;
- scepticism of rational-technical modes of practice;
- the recognition of power, powerlessness and empowerment;
- the development of genuine dialogue between users and those within the organisation, and within the organisation itself;
- attention to be paid to the fundamental purpose of the organisation and caution about becoming diverted into demonstrating productivity;
- the encouragement of openness, questioning, complaints and criticisms from outside and within the organisation;
- the removal of 'otherness' that may be attributed to those lower in the hierarchy, to users and to those relatively powerless in the community.

In this chapter we have considered the purposes of evaluation. We have looked briefly at the similarities and differences between evaluation, monitoring and research. And we have appraised the purposes of evaluation within notions of control, 'good' practice and preventing bad practice. We have concluded with a set of seven principles for evaluation for 'good' practice. With these in mind, and conscious of the dangers of evaluation being used and implemented as a means of control, we will, in the next chapter, look at theories of knowing employed in evaluation and test them for their appropriateness for an evaluation approach for 'good' practice.

3

Facts, Truth and Values

Case example

During negotiations that took place to set up the evaluation of the arts project in elderly persons' homes, the arts workers, and particularly the dance-and-movement worker, were very concerned that the external evaluator should not do what they thought of as a 'scientific' evaluation on them. This was not expressed as a reluctance to be evaluated. Far from it. The project, a voluntary one dependent on funding from both charitable sources and the local authority, was anxious to fulfil the evaluation requirement that was part of the condition of funding. But more important than that, the arts work for older people in residential care was established as a demonstration project and the workers were keen that it be evaluated so that learning from it could be captured and disseminated. The arts workers were convinced that their contribution improved the quality of living in residential care. They were committed to what they were doing, even passionate. It was thus important that the evaluation provided a way for their assumptions about the effectiveness of their work to be scrutinised.

The concerns expressed about evaluation stemmed from fears that a scientific model would be applied to the evaluation process and also, through this, to the process of practice. The dance-and-movement worker talked about evaluations that had been undertaken of similar work with older people where a medical approach to the work had been assumed by the evaluator. It had been assumed that improvement to quality of life meant making people better; that a measurable outcome of dance-and-movement work with older people would be improvements to physical movements. This she thought would deny important aspects of her work and of the intentions of the arts work and might even lead to negative conclusions. Such an evaluation would fail to capture the essence of the dance-and-movement sessions in the homes which was about older people and care workers together having fun, doing unexpected things, doing things that they thought they never could or should, expressing feelings that could not be articulated verbally. An evaluation that saw the intervention as treatment might conclude with no causal relationship between treatment and physical improvement. (Everitt, 1994)

Case example

Members of the area team of the social services department were keen to set up a team project that would provide opportunity to work together and to engage in preventive practice. They managed to get the training section to agree to them having a half-day away to review their work and develop plans. Through this process the team agreed to develop an innovatory piece of group work with young people leaving care. The social workers had expressed concern for some time about the lack of appropriate work and services for such young people on their caseloads. Many young people, both students from the local university and college and those who had been in care throughout the borough, came to live in the area in which the team was located, an inner-city area with a number of hostels and bed-sitters.

Following the half-day away, the team resolved to research their own practice, collect together data available about their area, and consult with NAYPIC (National Association for Young People in Care) and with the local university students' union about issues faced by young people. They did this over several months, a period of hard, but interesting and absorbing work that brought them together as a team and generated in them renewed feelings of commitment to policy and practice change. This work resulted in putting together a proposal for a group work project which would provide opportunity for young people leaving care and students to engage in dialogue together. The aim of the project was to contribute to young people becoming autonomous, able to live successfully in the community. The innovatory aspect of the project was to bring young people in different social, educational and employment situations, and having different levels of confidence and autonomy, together as peers.

With the support of the area team leader, the team submitted the proposal to a senior manager, requesting resources to cover staff costs, accommodation, refreshments and outings. This proposal eventually landed on the agenda of partnership planning meetings with one of the large national voluntary organisations.

Eventually, it was agreed that the social services department would provide accommodation for the project with the voluntary agency providing funding to cover all other costs for a three-year period. However, the aspect of the project involving students was not approved. Also, as a condition of the funding, the voluntary agency required that the project be evaluated. The team proposed that it do this themselves. Putting together the proposal had triggered off an interest in research. However, after considerable discussion, it was agreed that the project be evaluated by the research and development section of the Chief Executive's department. The team reluctantly agreed to this and to not including students. They were anxious to get the project off the ground and agreed with each other that, since the group work would be developmental, then students could be brought into the project at a later date.

The experience of the evaluation, however, made them vow never to enter into such a project again. The evaluator insisted on an evaluation design which had the effect of completely skewing the project. The team tried to persuade the evaluator to respect their ideas about the project and to fit in with the practice and allow the group to develop. The evaluator, though, had different ideas. For the purposes of the evaluation, young people leaving care were assigned to two groups: a control group and an experimental group. The evaluator interpreted being autonomous and living successfully as the same as having a steady job and keeping out of debt. The outputs which were used as measures of performance included such measurable factors as the number of job applications, interviews, length of time in employment, level of income, expenditure patterns, debts. The pressure on the team to succeed, measured by these yardsticks, was such that the group work turned into something quite different. The young people in the experimental group were required to attend a weekly session in which they were provided with information and skills in job searching, interview techniques, budgeting etc. It never was possible to develop the project in different ways by, for example, making links with young people who were students. The evaluator insisted that the intervention that was being measured had to remain unchanged during the period of the project. The members of the team became disillusioned and quite marginal to the project. Many of them did not even read the evaluation report when it was published and the team certainly did not consider it worth discussing.

These two examples of the relationship between practice and evaluation may sound familiar. The issues raised about evaluation, its purpose, its methodologies and its relationship to practice, reflect repeated criticisms that have been made of evaluation. These are summarised by Weiss, an evaluator, thus:

> there have been complaints about the lack of fit between evaluation and the socio-political context of the program world. Critics charge that evaluation is narrow because it focuses on only a small subset of questions of importance to program people; unrealistic because it measures the success of programs against unreasonably high standards; irrelevant because it provides answers to questions that no one really cares about; unfair because it is responsive to the concerns of influential people, such as bureaucratic sponsors, but blind to the wants of others lower in the hierarchy, such as front-line staff and

> clients; and unused in councils of action where decisions are made. (Weiss, 1986b: 145)

Evaluation is often experienced by practitioners as incompatible with the process and context of practice, as narrow, unrealistic, irrelevant, unfair and not useful to the making of policy and practice decisions. We would add a further criticism of evaluation which, while agreeing with the criticisms summarised by Weiss, to some extent contradicts them. It would appear that increasingly evaluation of a technical kind is being imposed on projects and on practice for reasons of policy and budgetary control. It is this concern about evaluation that we explore in this chapter.

The fears and the negative experiences of the practitioners in the case examples, we suggest, relate to the increasing use of evaluation in social welfare organisations as a form of policy control. In this scenario, evaluation is not 'irrelevant' as Weiss suggests, but rather highly relevant as one of the increasing array of strategies of managerialism and control of policy, practice and professionalism, in and across social welfare organisations. Evaluation here is not 'unused in councils of action where decisions are made' (Weiss, ibid.) but rather can be extremely useful in legitimising managerial and top-down decisions affecting and directing practice and policy development. Parton draws our attention to ways in which professionals, and the users of their services, are controlled through these processes:

> The increased emphasis on management, evaluation, monitoring, and constraining professionals to write things down, is itself a form of government of them, and more crucially, of those with whom they are working. It forces them to think about what they are doing and hence makes them accountable against certain norms. In the process, power flows to the centre or agent who determines the professionals' inscriptions,

> accumulates them, analyses them in their aggregate form, and can compare and evaluate the activities of others who are entries in the chart. (Parton, 1994a: 26)

In our analysis, we explore the relationship that there appears to be between, on the one hand, evaluation as part of the repertoire of managerial control and, on the other, particular styles of evaluation. We suggest that it is a particular approach to evaluation, a technical and supposedly value-free approach, that allows for its co-option by those who are powerful in shaping policies and allocating funds.

In the chapters that follow, we will look at alternative evaluation approaches that may be more relevant to our quest for a model that promotes 'good' practice. In this, we will look in more detail at the nature of practice, the responsibilities of the practitioner and the relationship between evaluation and practice change and development.

The developing use of evaluation

The policy research literature (for example, Weiss, 1977; Rein, 1976; Abt, 1978) traces the development of evaluation from the late 1950s and 60s when, particularly in the United States, it became a required component of federally funded and initiated social programmes. At that time, there was an optimism around about the part social science research could play in ensuring the effectiveness of policy programmes and processes in alleviating social problems and inequality. Programmes were set up as social experiments, with evaluation playing a major part in their design, documentation and their demonstrations of effectiveness. Social science, through evaluation, was seen as important in providing evidence of the effectiveness of these social experiments in order to feed back to the policy-makers and funding agencies. Notable amongst these were the

Headstart Programme, a pre-school initiative, and the War on Poverty programme (see Marris and Rein, 1967).

This model of social intervention and experimentation was replicated in the UK with the Educational Priority Areas (Halsey, 1974; Bulmer, 1986) and the Community Development Projects (CDPs) (National Community Development Project, 1973; Green, 1992). Social science research was attached to these projects in a variety of ways with the intention that it would inform policy decisions and action throughout the process of intervention: from the stages of problem definition and need assessment through to the evaluation of the effectiveness of interventions introduced. That the researchers in these projects did not necessarily do what was intended by their political sponsors (the Home Office and the Department of Education and Science) is part of the story of this book. In some parts of the CDP, the intended rational-technical model of research findings informing policy decisions prevailed. In these cases, researchers from the local university saw their role as providing analyses of social problems, needs and interventions for the community workers and for those in policy-making positions. They sought to remain separate from the practice. In making claims to neutrality and lack of bias in their research, they de-politicised the research process. In the 'radical' CDPs, however, researchers and community workers understood the research process as political.

> They explicitly chose to research the activities of the powerful in order to inform the efforts of working-class people to bring about changes in their life situations and chances . . . The use of research as facilitating social change at all levels was seen as paramount. (Green, 1992: 171)

The story of the CDP, and of this book, unravels the tale of evaluation as political as well as scientific, straddling both policy (and we include practitioners within policy processes) and research camps and involving complex and changing patterns of relationships between the two.

The early emphasis was therefore on evaluation as contributing to understandings of, and advising on changes to, social programmes to ensure their effectiveness. The later literature, in the 1970s and 80s, gives way to more pessimistic analyses in two major senses.

First, policy researchers and evaluators themselves have reflected on the lack of utilisation of research in policy-making processes (see, for example, Cronbach and Associates, 1980; Weiss, 1986a). They have pointed to the lack of fit between processes of research and evaluation, policy and development in practice. In this appraisal of the effectiveness of evaluation in informing policy decisions, the validity of what has been called the 'social engineering' model (Bulmer, 1982) has been questioned. In other words, policy researchers and evaluators have recognised that an approach to evaluation that assumes that those in policy-making and resource allocation positions are always open to be informed by research and evaluation findings, and act accordingly, is mistaken (Booth, 1988).

Policy decisions are made within social, economic and political processes in organisations. Organisations do not behave as rationally as their apolitical and atheoretical wall charts describing their structures would suggest. Policy initiatives and challenges come from all quarters, including from on high and from practitioners as 'street level bureaucrats' (Lipsky, 1980). Policy-making processes and decisions about the allocation of resources are political. Recognising that this is the context within which evaluation takes place, commentators on the effectiveness of evaluation have concluded that the utilisation of evaluation findings is a more diffuse process. The relationship between evaluation findings and learning from these findings is more indirect and multi-faceted than is acknowledged by the 'social engineering' model. We return to this debate about ways in which evaluation findings are utilised when we consider, in Chapter 8, the relationship between evaluation, policy and practice change and development.

The second strand of pessimism about evaluation and its utilisation relates to what might be termed an 'instrumental' approach to evaluation. In contrast to feeling negative because of the lack of influence that evaluation has in policy processes, there are those who are pessimistic precisely because of the ways in which evaluation is utilised by policy-makers. Rather than evaluation not being used, the picture unfolding today is of evaluation being misused.

The developing misuse of evaluation

> The new public management represents elements of neo-Taylorism with all the problems that scientific management models of the past have displayed (Pollitt, 1990). For example, it tends to argue that there is one best way to manage in all circumstances, that facts objectively measured speak for themselves, and that reward systems need to be linked to performance, however this is defined. All these claims are debatable not necessarily because they are ipso facto wrong, but because they conceal assumptions that need to be examined. (Gray and Jenkins, 1993: 22–3)

Thus, the perceived gap between evaluation and management that so concerned policy researchers of the 1970s and 80s has been effectively closed by the instrumental co-option of 'scientific' evaluation for 'scientific' management. The approach to evaluation that produces facts, measured through supposedly objective procedures, facts that can 'speak for themselves', instrumentally serves the purpose of managerialism. Such evaluations serve to legitimate supposedly objective management decisions to cut and privatise services. We are then assured that these decisions are based on 'scientific' facts.

This, we suggest, is the basis of the fears of evaluation and alienation from evaluation presented by the practitioners at the beginning of this chapter. It is a basis with some foundation. In the remainder of this chapter, we explore in more detail this 'scientific' evaluation and show how, because of its technocratic approach, it is ripe for co-option for political purposes. Not wanting to fall into the trap of seeing managers as 'baddies' and practitioners as 'goodies', in Chapter 5 we reflect on ways in which practitioners too can be instrumental in their use of evaluation.

Evaluation and the scientific method

The concerns of the practitioners in the arts project and the area team introduced at the beginning of this chapter were about an approach to evaluation where:

- the evaluator is separate from the practitioners and from the practice supposedly in order to ensure neutrality and objectivity;
- practice is conceptualised as informed by a medical/treatment model with defined inputs and measurable outcomes;
- causal relationships are sought between inputs and outputs;
- different interventions are applied to control and experimental groups so that differences in outcomes can be measured and compared, and these differences are then related in causal ways to differences in inputs;
- interventions in the control and experimental groups are controlled for the period of the project so that measurements can be made, thus not allowing for practice as a developing and changing process;
- decisions are made about intended outputs depending on their susceptibility to measurement, thus simpli-

fying what otherwise may be complex, diffuse and multi-faceted goals and processes.

Evaluation is about generating evidence of practice and its effectiveness. The approach described above is one way of doing this. It is an approach informed by positivist ideas about social science, its methodology and methods. Within this paradigm, social scientific research is understood as akin to the classical paradigms of natural and physical sciences. Emphasis is placed on the researcher, or the evaluator, remaining separate from that which is being evaluated to ensure both their own neutrality and the objectivity of data collected. Practice is set up as if in a laboratory, certainly within controlled conditions, so that it may be measured and other possible influences upon it either eliminated or taken into account. Assumptions are made that the elements of practice, and their effects, can be measured. Quantitative and statistical techniques are applied for measurement and for analysis. The aim is to draw conclusions that this input, this intervention, causes, or does not cause, this outcome. Input and outcome variables are measured and their relationship with each other analysed statistically. With conclusions about causality, predictions may be made to the effect that, if implemented, the intervention will generate particular outcomes. The opposite may also be predicted, i.e. that these interventions will not generate these outcomes. These are the facts that 'speak for themselves'.

The literature on evaluation often assumes that its purpose is to establish causal relationships. Phillips, Palfrey and Thomas (1994), for example, in their otherwise useful and accessible guide to methods of evaluation, start with defining evaluation

> as concerned with judging merit against some yardstick. It involves the collection, analysis and interpretation of data bearing on the achievement of an organisation's goals and

> programme objectives. Evaluation usually attempts to measure the extent to which certain outcomes can be validly correlated with inputs and/or outputs. The aim is to establish whether there is a cause–effect relationship. (Phillips, Palfrey and Thomas, 1994: 1)

The aim of evaluation is not 'to establish whether there is a cause–effect relationship'. The aim of evaluation is to judge merit.

Values and the scientific method

The fundamental belief of positivist social science is that facts, and the collection and analyses of these, may be separated from values. Thus, evaluation supposedly produces results about effectiveness that are clear and unequivocal. Such evaluators claim that they are able to discover the truth of practice through demonstrating causal relations:

> Perhaps more clearly than any other research strategy, conclusions can be drawn as to the presence or absence of the intervention being the likely explanation for observed differences in outcome. (Cheetham *et al.*, 1992: 25)

However, within the social sciences, it is now largely accepted that 'facts' are constructed through social processes. Science does not produce the truth. It produces a version of reality and can be helpful in providing ways to systematically scrutinise those things which we have come to know so well that we take them for granted, no longer giving them even a passing thought. It can provide evidence that serves to nudge us into thinking differently. It can provoke us into searching for the reasons why we think and choose to act in particular ways. But science does not provide us with value-free facts and truths about the world; at its best, it points to probabilities. It does not produce the answers. And nor do scientists. Scientists, and evaluators, are not free of values, no more than anyone else is. Their perspectives on the world are shaped through their experiences just as is the case for all of us. True, the nature of their craft is to provide evidence in ways that are rigorous, systematic and accountable. This does not mean, though, that values can be eliminated from the process.

Who decides on the evaluation? For what purposes? At what time? In what depth? All these contain within them value decisions. Who does the evaluation? In what ways? For whom? On what? The answers demand that value judgements be made. What questions are asked? Of whom? In what ways? What questions are not asked? All are imbued with values. The process of generating evidence about practice and its effects is imbued with values. To resort to supposed neutrality and objectivity is to fail to make prevailing values explicit. It is an approach that masks values which are integral to the process and therefore makes them not amenable to scrutiny, accountability and possibly change.

This is true of research and evaluation. But in evaluation the place of values is even more significant. Evaluation is not only a means of generating evidence about practice. It also involves placing a value on practice. It entails making decisions about the value of practice informed with evidence generated in systematic and rigorous ways. The scientific method, and other methods for generating evidence, must not be conflated with the processes of making judgements about the worth of the practice. Evaluations within the positivist paradigm often collapse these two very distinct, although interrelated, elements into one; that of producing evidence, on the one hand, and of judgement-making about the 'good', on the other. It is assumed that since evaluation results represent the truth of practice and its achievements, then there is no need to make judgements on the basis of values.

The politics of evaluation

The powerful alliance between 'scientific' rational-technical management and technocratic evaluation treats 'facts as speaking for themselves'. Findings are presented by such evaluators as almost certainly true, allowing for probability. Those wanting to use such evaluation findings to legitimise policy preferences, such as cutting the budget to a project, have the choice to accept or reject findings from the evaluation. If they agree with them, if the findings support decisions they want to make, then they can be treated as factual, as 'scientific', as truth. If the findings though do not provide the necessary support, then either they can be treated as only probable or the evaluator can be accused of being biased and of allowing values to enter the process. Either way, making the evaluation process technical and treating the utilising of evaluation findings as technical acknowledges no place, or rather, no need, for judgement-making about the 'good'. Judgements about the 'good' are treated as self-evident.

Having established the integral relationship between evaluation and values, this pretence at sticking to the facts merely masks the place of values and judgements about the 'good' contained within the process:

> Evaluation very much involves values . . . The value-free stance adopted by many researchers and evaluators – such as merely collecting information and letting administrators value it as they will – is completely wrong. (House, 1986: 51)

In recognising that neither management nor evaluation are value-free, we are alerted to understanding the alliance between neo-Taylorism in management and rational-technical evaluation as political. Technical approaches to management and evaluation serve to hide judgements about value, about the 'good', and therefore remove them from the public arena and from debate.

Causality and evaluation

Our approach to evaluation is not one that rejects scientific methods. Nor do we reject the quest for causality out of hand. Our concern is twofold. First, the seemingly increasing extent to which evaluations are depoliticised, undertaken as rational-technical exercises and then used instrumentally by those controlling the policy-making arenas in which resources are allocated, budgets cut, some projects favoured over others, causes us concern. And second, the extent to which causality is emphasised and even treated as the aim of evaluation provides the opportunity for such processes of de-politicisation and instrumentalism.

The design of any evaluation must take account of the practice to be evaluated, its purposes and policy contexts, and the purposes of the evaluation. We recognise that there may be times when those involved in the practice agree upon an experimental or quasi-experimental approach as the most appropriate way of generating and analysing evidence of effectiveness. This will depend on the practice that is to be evaluated, the extent to which objectives of the practice can be pre-defined and measured, and the state of existing knowledge about the effectiveness of the practice.

Oakley (1990), for example, makes a cogent reply to those who have dismissed, on practical and ethical grounds, 'scientific' evaluations of pre-natal health care. She appraises such evaluations and expresses concern about the reluctance to hold controlled trials to find out whether particular interventions and programmes work. She argues for randomised controlled trials (where two similar groups are compared, one receiving the programme intervention, the other not) in situations where there exists uncertainty about the effectiveness of the intervention. The interventions to which she refers have very clear intended and measurable outcomes. Oakley also reminds us that not to know about the effectiveness of programmes, or to rely only on practitioners' and policy-makers' hunches and beliefs, and yet to continue to implement them and allocate resources to them, is irresponsible, in resource terms and ultimately in life or death terms. Experimental designs have their place in evaluations, but need to be interrogated. Causality can become so prominent that the meaning of evaluation as making judgements about good practice is lost or rather is hidden within technical expertise and decision-making.

> Evaluation is not a search for cause and effect, an inventory of present status, or a prediction of future success. It is something of all of these but only as they contribute to understanding substance, function and worth. (Stake and Denny, 1969: 370)

While Stake and Denny (1969) do not reject the search for causality, say for making causal connections between input and outcomes, they insist that evaluation is more than this. There is a need to be critical of evaluations which claim to produce conclusive findings about the effectiveness of practice. It is important to be cautious about the temptation to treat such claims as truth and to regard the scientific method as having replaced the essential process of judgement-making about the 'good'.

Returning to the case examples at the opening of this chapter, the arts workers and the members of the area team were both concerned that the expert, external and supposedly neutral evaluator should not be the one to make judgements about effectiveness. The arts workers approached their initial discussions with the evaluator with concerns that the process of such judgement-making about the practice would be taken away from them. They anticipated that, within the 'scientific' evaluation paradigm, the practice would fail to show any measurable effects in terms of making people better. And that furthermore, the 'good' things about the practice would not be appreciated.

The area team members found that the evaluation took away from them the processes of judgement-making about effectiveness. In drawing up outcome measures, the evaluator in effect exerted considerable influence on the practice. Both the arts workers and the social workers were aware of the power of 'science' in evaluation and were anxious to retain the making of judgements about the practice. They were both convinced that what they were doing, or were planning, was 'good'. Questions, of course, need to be raised not only about the place of the supposedly neutral evaluator in the processes of judgement-making, but also the place of highly committed and convinced practitioners. We suggest that neither has a prerogative in the making of judgements about value. The practitioner however has a professional responsibility to ensure that evaluation is undertaken for the purpose of moving towards 'good' practice and is implemented through processes that themselves will enhance the possibilities of 'good' practice.

Evaluating for 'good' practice

Returning to the principles we set for ourselves at the end of the previous chapter for appraising evaluation approaches for their ability to ensure 'good' practice, the technical approach to evaluation that we have been referring to in this chapter falls far short of our aspirations.

- Moral debate about practice is important and everybody, irrespective of power, status and position, has the right to legitimate opinions.

There is no place in rational-technical evaluations for moral debate. Opinions are treated as evidence of input or output. They are not legitimate in themselves but are analysed as objective data. Power, status and position in the shaping of opinion, and in the design, implementation and use of evaluations, are not acknowledged. Because of the need for expertise, the evaluator as 'independent expert' can easily assume or be attributed more power, status and position than other participants in the evaluation process.

- There is a need to be sceptical of the rational-technical mode of thinking and operating.

The analysis in this chapter has illustrated the dangers of the rational-technical mode in silencing debate about effectiveness and 'good' practice. Furthermore, we have suggested that such approaches to evaluation can be misused to serve the policy preferences and funding priorities of the powerful.

- Power and powerlessness corrupt. Everybody should be consulted about whether practice is effective in ways that take account of power and powerlessness.

Notions of power are irrelevant to technical evaluation to such an extent that the power of the evaluator and those who have commissioned the evaluation are not acknowledged. Nor is power and powerlessness taken into account in the process of attaching meaning to data generated. Data and evidence are treated as objective, existing independently of social and powerful processes and structures.

- Dialogue involving users and practitioners is essential to the process of critically commenting on effectiveness and 'good' practice.

People engage little with rational-technical evaluations. Managers and/or funders may commission the evaluation and appoint the evaluators. They, with other workers in the organisation, may be consulted about the design of the evaluation and encouraged to participate. Participation by workers and users will be confined to providing data. Knowledge of the evaluation process and its findings will rest with the evaluator as independent expert who will impart it to others, differentially according to their position in the organisation. Communication is skewed in one direction: from evaluator to others.

- Technically achievable and measurable objectives should not take the place of acknowledging and debating the fundamental purpose of the project or practice.

An evaluation geared to establishing causal relationships between inputs and outcomes will take for granted the fundamental purpose of the project or practice. The relevance of the inputs and outcomes to this purpose, and the extent to which they express the values contained within this purpose, will not be questioned or seen as relevant to such an evaluation.

- Evaluative organisations should strive towards openness, valuing questioning of their policies and practices, and responsive to complaints and criticisms.

The encouragement of openness in the organisation and its receptiveness is not seen as the province of technical evaluations. On the contrary, the 'scientific' method and expertise of the evaluator may serve to mystify the process. It may divert critical thinking about and within the organisation into technical processes open only to experts.

- There are dangers in processes that objectify users and practitioners, treating them as 'other', denying their experiences and views as having any credibility and legitimacy.

Evaluations undertaken within a positivist paradigm objectify others in the interests of neutrality. Workers and users will be related to only as data providers. Depending on the extent to which findings are used to legitimise particular policy and practice preferences, practitioners and projects will be required to make changes.

Concluding this chapter, then, we do not dismiss causal evaluations within a positivist paradigm. They have their place, particularly when programme interventions can be clearly defined and documented and when intended outcomes are equally clear and measurable. We do, though, reject the apparent sovereignty of the positivist, rational-technical approach to evaluation. We are fearful of its compatibility with 'managerial evaluation' and therefore of its strengthening of evaluation for control and its peripheral relationship with the endeavour to ensure 'good' practice.

However, nor do we simply go along with the beliefs of practitioners and their organisations and projects, no matter how passionate and committed these may be. We will proceed to look at alternative ways to get to know about practice and to make judgements about whether it is 'good' or 'good enough'. The arts workers were convinced that their contribution improved the quality of living in residential care. They were committed to what they were doing, even passionate. But they may be mistaken, carried along with their enthusiasms and their way of seeing things. It is important that evaluation provides a way for the assumptions of practitioners about the effectiveness of their work to be scrutinised. Practitioners too may use evaluation instrumentally.

Having looked in more detail, in the next chapter, at the growth and use of performance indicators in social welfare, we then proceed by looking at alternative approaches to evaluation that may fit more with the repertoire of the practitioner.

4

Measuring Performance

Performance measurement has been a central plank in the drive for value for money and accountability in public services. As we suggested in the previous chapter, it is largely through mechanisms of performance measurement that evaluation has become integral to new forms of public sector management. In this chapter we appraise the nature of these developments and explore them for the scope they offer in developing evaluation for good practice.

Performance measurement and performance indicators

'Performance measurement' is a generic term suggesting that a mosaic of indicators be used to evaluate a service.

> Performance measurement is a coherent collation of information on aspects of services provided and about those needing, seeking or receiving these. The information should constitute a selection of 'measures' which derive from an explicit statement of values and objectives and should relate directly to an assessment of whether these values and objectives are being met. (Barnes and Miller, 1988: 17)

Measures may be developed through service management information, performance indicators, one-off reviews, user surveys and reports of inspections. If standards are unambiguous, performance measures may be relatively precise, like reading data from a dial such as levels of water purity.

'Performance indicator' is used as a generic term to describe sets of statistics which may show how well or badly a service is doing, without providing explanations (Cohen, 1989: 14). Frequently, there is no precise interpretation of these data, so performance indicators are viewed as 'alarm bells' or 'tin openers'. They are provocative and suggestive, indicating the need for further exploration (Jackson, 1988a: 11). For example, if per pupil costs in one school are three times greater than those in another, this is not a measure that one school is thrice more efficient than the other. Rather, it indicates that further exploration is necessary.

Performance measures and indicators should be used comparatively. Several services may be compared simultaneously or changes in one service examined over time.

Case example

Measuring the performance of services for children under five

Performance Measurement Category	Performance Indicators
1. Financial	Net spending of local authority. Net *SSD spending per capita.
2. Needs in the community	% population under 5. No. of under-5s in main ethnic group. % of households overcrowded.
3. SSDs' policies and objectives	Priority to under-5s (% of SSD spending). Support for vulnerable parents/children (staff contact time with parents).
4. External factors	Involvement of Health and Education Services.
5. Service functions	No. of places in nurseries

	(local authority, private, voluntary).
6. Service users	% of children in main ethnic group in local authority in nurseries, playgroups.
7. Service components	% of local authority staff in under-5s services.
8. Quality of resource inputs	% turnover of staff. % of trained staff from ethnic minorities.
9. Use pattern	No. of children starting during year – local authority nurseries.
10. Client and carers' satisfaction	Survey data.
11. Unit costs and charges	Gross unit cost per week per place. Charge per week per place.
12. Substitutable services	% NSPCC nursery places.

(extracted from Cohen, 1989)

* SSD – Local Authority Social Services Department.

Frameworks for measuring performance

If measuring performance assesses whether the values of a service are accorded with and/or its objectives met, some attempt must be made to identify these values and objectives. This goes to the very heart of theory and practice in social welfare. The following case example illustrates a process of teasing out the values and objectives, what may be termed 'purpose', in child protection services.

Case example

Hardiker and Barker (1994a) provide evidence of ways in which one local authority successfully implemented the values and objectives of the children's services. These were derived from:

- The principles underlying the 1989 Children Act: child's welfare paramount, non-interventionism, parental responsibility and partnership with families; legal threshold criteria; legal requirements; no delay; addressing cultural, religious and ethnic issues; orders in all proceedings.
- The objectives outlined in a social services department's child care strategy: the welfare principle; the importance of families; the least intrusive intervention; parental involvement in decision-making; taking account of the child's wishes and feelings; non-discriminatory services and practices; the continuum of care; the rights of children.
- The values, knowledge and skills of the practitioners engaged in child protection and implementing the new legislation.

'Value for money' frameworks may be used as another yardstick to evaluate the values and objectives of social welfare services in terms of economy, efficiency and effectiveness. These criteria may be used to measure the quality of a service's performance through the use of:

- cost indicators to measure economy
- productivity indicators to measure efficiency
- quality of service indicators to measure effectiveness.

Knapp (1989) discusses the prospects for developing performance measures in relation to outcomes in child care, starting with the following wise caveat:

> Little is known about the impacts of child care interventions in child, family and social welfare, still less about how best to measure them and a plurality of methodologies is needed. (Knapp, 1989: 27)

Knapp develops a 'production of welfare' framework which has five components:

- Resource inputs: staff, physical, capital, provisions and other consumables;
- Non-resource inputs: personalities, activities and attitudes of staff;
- Intermediate outcomes: measures of quality of care rather than quality of life;
- Final outcomes: changes in child welfare, defined in terms of society's objectives for child care and child development.
- Throughputs and processes: child care practices.

Knapp points out that this production process is interactional and dynamic rather than static and mechanistic. External factors, such as 'who is the client?', are also relevant. For example, evaluation questions in respect of incarcerating adolescent delinquents need to recognise that

> the needs of society for protection or punishment may outweigh the prospects of serious detrimental effects for the adolescents concerned. Indeed, the differences themselves say a great deal about the effectiveness of child care. (Knapp, 1989: 197)

Referring back to the performance measures and indicators for services for children under five outlined on pages 58–9, the components of Knapp's 'production of welfare model' are clearly in evidence:

• Contextual:	1.	financial
	2.	needs in the community
	4.	external factors
	7.	service components
	12.	substitutable services
• Input:	5.	service functions
	7.	service components
	8.	quality of resource inputs

• Process:	6.	service users
• Outcome:	9.	use pattern
	10.	client and carers' satisfaction
	11.	unit costs and charges

As Knapp suggests, it is always important to examine every component in the model. These facilitate measures of economy, efficiency and effectiveness, which in turn provide a methodology for accountability in child care services. It appears that Knapp, in taking account of both process and external factors, has taken on board some of the limitations of positivist input–output models in his 'production of welfare' framework.

Measuring performance as a means of control

The growth of performance indicators in public services has been fuelled by

> a long crusade to introduce more rational techniques into government . . . ; . . . the sustained political commitment of the Thatcher government to containing the growth in public expenditure . . .; and the recent diffusion of cheap information technology. (Carter, 1988a: 369)

Significant implicit assumptions underlying these social changes may be revealed by relating them to models of organisations. Palpably embedded in the criteria of economy, efficiency and effectiveness are notions about the rationality of social welfare agencies. These are also evident in assumptions about the use of performance measurement to identify the extent to which services are achieving the values and objectives of the agency. The question this leaves us with is the extent to which meaningful performance indicators can be developed if organisations do not function as rationally as the model implies.

The political requirement for central control of decentralised, fragmentary services operating in a market economy leaves government with a paradox. Carter suggests one answer:

> In order to overcome the familiar organisational paradox, that to decentralise it is necessary to centralise, the government has encouraged the development of performance indicators as a 'hands off' instrument of control over service delivery. (Carter, 1988a: 131)

To retain control and accountability of decentralised units, government needs to be able to state explicitly the form, quantity and quality of inputs, outputs and outcomes expected from them. However, it is often impossible to establish what departments are accomplishing (Carter, 1989). The introduction of performance indicators is an answer which, however, proved difficult given the inadequacies of existing information and measurement systems. The Financial Management Initiative (FMI) outlined in Chapter 1 was one attempt to solve this problem by developing a 'hands off' system of control. A range of responses has emerged to address such central government attempts to control organisations and practices through either backseat driving or hands-off systems.

Data-driven indicators have been produced by public service managers responding to directives about performance indicators and producing readily available data. Examples of these include: personnel statistics or simple measures of activity such as numbers of recipients of social security benefits, crimes cleared up, number of outpatients treated. Easy-to-measure outputs have been adopted by local Social Security offices: clearance times and error rates. Our concern is that, through the use of such measures of performance, the purposes of social welfare may be usurped or displaced if systems are assumed to be more rational than they are.

Perhaps it was the assumption of rationality in organisations which was one of the problems experienced in, and emanating from, the implementation of such initiatives! If so, different models of organisations should inform models of performance measurement. One alternative, an interactionist approach, suggests that the focus could be upon the front-line workers, 'street level bureaucrats' (Lipsky, 1980), who implement the policies, values and objectives of agencies. Indicators then may be linked to objectives set by street-level bureaucrats in the process of solving their problems. This raises the debate about whether decisions about indicators are matters for professional judgement or for supposedly rational-technical management. Both cases clearly raise issues about accountability for standards: professional, technical/managerial, or democratic.

Furthermore, within New Right managerialist performance measurement, efficiency is measured as the ratio of inputs to outputs, though the links between these are not always clear (Carter, 1988a). For example, the Department of Social Security compared administrative costs to benefits paid out; the Inland Revenue calculated the amount of tax contributions collected per staff member; the NHS worked out the number of hospital patients per bed.

Finally, performance indicators may be available but not used by practitioners and managers. For example, MPs have far more information than they can handle and parliamentary questions rarely are asked even when well-established indicators are available (Carter, 1988a). Sometimes, managers develop their own PIs which seem more pertinent for their tasks than those imposed upon them. Some universities, for example, have developed their own administrative performance indicators.

Crude as they may be sometimes, decentralised units still need to operationalise performance indicators. Progress, though, in terms of useful indicators for evaluating 'good' practice, is bound to be slow for a variety of reasons (Carter, 1989).

First, many decentralised units do not 'own' numerous aspects of their performance, especially when external factors impinge on this. For example, crime levels are a function of social and economic factors as well as police crime-prevention policies, and social class factors affect educational performances. Inter-agency relations have a bearing on the performance of some services: sentencing policies on prison populations; housing policies on health; hospital discharge policies on community care. If it is difficult to identify the contribution of one unit to its own performance, how much more difficult is it to measure the impact of external influences on the performance of a social welfare service?

Second, it is difficult to relate performance to precise objectives because these are invariably multiple, ambiguous, conflicting, vague and displaced. For example, the 1989 Children Act is very precise about the use of 'accommodation' and a social services department may formulate very precise policies about this in its child care strategy. However, it may still be difficult to identify performance in respect of the throughput of children accommodated in relation to these objectives. Accommodation may be used for many different purposes, such as social protection and social control and not just as an ordinary service following the wishes of a child's parents.

Third, professional ideologies may be very resistant to what are perceived as forms of political and managerial control. Professionals regard themselves as accountable to their peers rather than to managers and sponsors. Consequently, surgeons, judges and university lecturers assert their autonomy by using strategic performance indicators, such as hours spent in the theatre, court or classroom (Carter, 1989).

To recapitulate, rational approaches to organisations

implicit in performance measurement have elicited a number of responses not all that meaningful to the task of evaluating for 'good' practice. Social welfare organisations and projects have produced data that are readily available so that indicators are data-driven rather than linked to clear sets of objectives. Efficiency has often been measured through simple input/output ratios. Some have developed their own performance indicators. Responses such as these often have come about because many organisations, or decentralised units, do not 'own' their performance and objectives are invariably multiple, conflicting and ambiguous. The autonomy of professionals has also sometimes subverted the political and managerial controls implied by performance indicators.

We shall now explore the prospects for further developments in performance measurement. In this we take as our starting point that the purpose of social welfare, its values and objectives, are contestable, political and difficult to operationalise.

Ways forward in performance measurement

To develop more meaningful ways to measure performance in order to ensure 'good' practice, the hiatus between bureaucratic-rational and interactionist/front-line approaches to organisations has to be addressed. Hardiker, Exton and Barker (1991a) argue that an approach is needed that will explain the ways in which organisations survive in their environments and daily manage to produce the outputs of policies. They indicate that systems approaches enable us to explore points in the policy process whereby the authoritative intentions of policy-makers and the activities of practitioners are brought together:

> This approach treats policies as identifiable phenomena even though they may be heterogeneous, partial, unclear and con-

> tradictory. Room is allowed for the analysis of practitioners' contributions to policies. (Hardiker *et al.*, 1991a: 71)

> In order to survive in their environments, organisations 'need' to exchange problems for resources and convert inputs into outputs. These processes are facilitated by various structures: interdependence between different points, such as production and marketing or services and resources; boundaries between the organisation and its environment, such as social service committees or arrangements for client access. The effect of these structures and processes may be viewed as a series of balancing acts or a managed equilibrium, which adjust authoritative intentions and front-line activity. (Hardiker *et al.*, 1991a: 71)

Thus, the responses of social welfare organisations and projects, and their practitioners, to some of the requirements of performance measurement are not necessarily acts of sabotage or deviance by autonomous workers. Rather, they may contribute to systems of control which can be owned and shared by all relevant constituencies. At the same time, in developing a critical approach to evaluation we recognise the need to take account of the ways in which power and powerful processes operate in organisations.

We now explore this argument in three ways:

- developing methods for purposes;
- overcoming technical obstacles;
- addressing who is the client.

Methods for purposes

Different models of organisations may be relevant for different purposes. Hoyes *et al.* (1992) helpfully argue that different assumptions about the nature of organisations may be relevant for different dimensions of the production of welfare model:

- a rational approach may be relevant for measuring input/output ratios and final outputs;
- an interactionist approach may be relevant in understanding processes and throughputs.

A critical approach, the focus of this book, would be relevant to understanding both the products and processes of practice. It would differ from the other two approaches in its attention to power. A critical approach takes account of power in the processes of generating evidence of practice, in quantitative and qualitative forms, and in the processes of making judgements about whether the practice is good or not. Furthermore, an approach informed by critical theories of knowledge would be concerned not only with measuring performance and developing understandings, but also with ensuring that these processes generate change in the direction of the 'good'. We develop this critical approach in more detail in the following chapter.

Overcoming technical obstacles

Some of the responses to performance measurement set out above relate to the slow development of information technology in many social welfare organisations and projects (Hoyes *et al.*, 1992). Hoyes *et al.* illustrate ways in which several local authority social services departments have overcome some of these technical obstacles in relation to community care. However, they have found performance measures still to be wanting. For example, they suggest that the baseline data provided by the Chartered Institute of Public Finance and Accountancy (CIPFA), the Department of Health and supplementary information from local authorities were limited because:

- the data have not been of the right type to inform policy-makers about objectives being met;

- data have not facilitated the making of valid comparisons between authorities;
- data have not enabled changes over time in individual authorities to be traced and explained.

Hoyes *et al.* suggest that the baseline data produced by authorities have also often been weak because:

- the data related to services provided by social services departments only, excluding the services of other agencies;
- data related to service inputs and outputs rather than processes and outcomes;
- the indicators had little rational basis because clear statements of policies and objectives were lacking;
- little indication was provided of the impact of policy changes upon users and carers.

They conclude that without the requisite evidence, it is difficult to compare

> a quasi-market approach to service provision with the previous bureaucratic systems of resource allocation. (Hoyes *et al.*, 1992: 57)

The weakness in these information systems reflects all the issues about performance measurement that we have already identified: the requirement to identify the purpose of the service; the need to use a comparative approach; the importance in taking account of external factors, including the work of other agencies; the need to measure the impact of effectiveness.

There are many examples of performance indicators being developed in the criminal justice system (Carter, 1988b):

- The Lord Chancellor's Department introduced a set

of circuit objectives in 1984, using the trial as the basic unit of measurement. Waiting time for committals, sentencing and dispositions of appeals are used as straightforward throughput measures; the daily use secured from court rooms is used as an intermediate output measure. Few output data are produced.

- The Prison Department has also developed the use of performance indicators. Objectives of the service are identified and related to the function of units; governors have a weekly monitoring system related to the delivery of services, activities and routines; use is made of simple and reliable key indicators of intermediate outputs, such as a successful completion of routines and explanations for shortfalls.
- The police use personnel returns for inputs and clear-up rates for crime for outputs.

Finally, Carter *et al.* (1991) have undertaken a comparative study of fourteen government departments, public agencies and private business. They found that the most effective performance indicators were bespoke, timely and parsimonious. Differences between organisations in these respects did not mirror the public/private divide. The complexity of the NHS on every political, administrative and service delivery dimension explains why their performance indicators are less effective, i.e. data-driven, slow and promiscuous.

These selected examples suggest that the ultimate goal of political control through performance indicators is unattainable in absolute terms. The constant negotiations which apparently take place in respect of setting objectives, back-seat driving and hands-off controls, data-driven responses, front-line strategies, etc., illustrate the need for a middle-range level of analysis and practice in the development of performance indicators. Before we address this issue, we shall briefly explore the important question in any evaluation: who is the client?

Who is the client?

Whether the users of public services are described as customers, consumers or clients, the question of who they are is fundamental. As Carter *et al.* (1991) argue, the consumers of police services are those who have to call on them for help and those who expect them to maintain an environment in which their help is not required. The consumers of the NHS are those using the services and those who look upon them as an insurance against the time when they might have an acute illness. As we outlined above, the children's services serve the therapeutic needs of young people in trouble and the needs of society for protection, punishment and retribution. The clients of voluntary welfare agencies may be their sponsors whose gifts bestow an element of social control and beneficence (Jones, 1991).

Pollitt (1988) argues that early developments in performance measurement gave little priority to consumer perspectives, mainly because many approaches were in the rational positivist, managerial, top-down tradition. In contrast, the consumerism of the New Right gave some priority to users and citizens, especially in relation to public services. This could be interpreted as a move towards a more interactionist, bottom-up approach to evaluation. However, a theoretical analysis of such developments taking account of power reveals the underlying motive and experience of many of these as cosmetic, emphasising customer relations and signposting services rather than being genuinely participatory and power sharing.

There are limitations to user empowerment, though, in relation to performance measurement.

- First, consumerism will increase the pressures on public service managers, especially when they are expected to provide very sensitive information, not readily available, to a self-interested and unpredictable public (Pollitt, 1988: 78).

- Second, as we have seen, the consumers of a service may not be readily identifiable at a specific point in time.
- Third, public services are distinctive in that they are allocated according to political and bureaucratic rather than market criteria – for example, defence, street lighting and environmental health services. In other words, services may not be provided for identified users but rather for the benefit of society as a whole.
- Fourth, users of public services may have a statutory right to them, they may be involuntary clients or they may be given low priority through targeting.
- Fifth, vulnerable people and groups are not necessarily well served by market-driven criteria.
- Finally, consumers may be seen as citizens with expectations of equal opportunities, representation and participation in services. However, citizens have not exactly participated yet in the design and use of performance indicators.

To summarise, there have been many developments in the use of performance measures which can facilitate evaluation in social welfare services by generating evidence of practice. Different approaches may be relevant for different purposes: a rational-positivist one in relation to inputs and outputs; a more interactionist one in respect of processes. But whatever the approach to generating evidence of practice and its achievements, in social welfare it should be informed by an analysis of power. Some of the technical obstacles may have been overcome, especially with developments in information technology. Nevertheless, many performance indicators are still too data-driven, providing simple measures of activity, input and output. Finally, the question of who is the client raises all the political, theoretical, organisational and technical issues identified throughout this chapter. This question will not go away.

We now explore the prospects for developments in performance measurement, as a prelude to exploring their relevance for evaluating 'good' practice.

Prospects for development

Hoyes *et al.* (1992) suggest that common ground between rational-positivist and interactionist-interpretivist approaches to performance measurement may be found in developmental processes:

- Outcomes cannot always be analysed through rational methods based upon experimental designs. Therefore, performance indicators need to be developed to test progress during implementation phases, based upon participatory approaches. For example, intermediate outputs may be used as proxies for final outcomes: number of patients treated as proxies for the health of the population; examination results for improved education of the population.
- The pluralist interactionist evaluator may present interesting theories of compromise in the process of policy implementation. Similarly, developmental methods may enable observers to take sides rather than merely describe the seamless web of activities by street-level bureaucrats. Information and evidence may then be fed back into the programme for facilitating the process of choice clarification and judgements about 'good' or 'poor' practices (see Whitmore, 1991).

Such a problem-solving approach to high performance management should aid policy and priority formation, implementation, monitoring and control (Goold and Campbell, 1987; Jackson 1988a). This approach has the following advantages (Jackson, 1988a):

- defining goals helps to set priorities and helps managers and others involved in the organisation to grasp how it fits together in delivering its outputs;
- defining objectives, goals and targets assists in motivating individuals;
- if goals are unclear, the allocation of resources may be arbitrary and driven by vested or preferential interests;
- if individuals know that they have successfully achieved their goal, their morale improves.

The political and structural contexts of social welfare organisations often set boundaries to problem-solving approaches like those just outlined. For example, Gunn (1978) suggests the following as ideal preconditions for successful policy implementation:

- ensure that the central messages of the policy are unambiguous;
- create simple implementation structures with few links in the chain;
- minimise external influences;
- control front-line workers.

However, the goals of social welfare, of children's and community care services for example, are complex, often contradictory and contested. Their political economy requires complex chains of accountability. External influences, quite rightly, may put the most tightly managed organisations off course. For example, the rise of child abuse referrals to many social services departments during the 1980s distorted many supposedly rational child care strategies. The rise in the prison population has had very serious consequences for performance in that service. Finally, the activities of practitioners cannot always be, nor should they be, as finely tuned as performance measures require.

Nevertheless, developments have moved on apace in social welfare organisations. In social services departments, central government guidance and regulations give greater specificity to the goals of new legislation. Policy implementation chains have been strengthened through requirements for inspection, review and written procedures. Many organisations have attempted to minimise external influences and control their workloads through gatekeeping, priority setting and tightly specifying target groups. The discretion of practitioners has been bounded by: the legal requirements of 1989 Children Act; systems for assessing need and devising community care plans; strict guidelines for pre-sentence reports in the probation service. Voluntary organisations are being controlled through contracting, service specifications and output measurement.

There is no going back!

Performance indicators will continue to be developed and used as a tool for monitoring social welfare services. As a means of controlling and replacing what perhaps should be democratic and research-minded processes in organisations, they are a cause for concern. At the same time, they can be useful in generating evidence of the practice in terms of its inputs and intended outputs and outcomes. The development of process indicators, thus not relying solely on measures of pre-set outputs, may be reassuring to practitioners. They provide the opportunity to generate evidence of the processes of providing services in a principled, competent and caring manner.

It is now important to develop a critical approach to ways of measuring performance that takes account of analyses of power. There are problems when rational and interactionist (or positivist and interpretivist) approaches are used to the exclusion of each other. And, as we reveal in the next chapter, neither of these approaches takes on board dimensions of power through which data and evidence of practice, including measures of performance, are constructed.

If performance measurement is to progress as a means of generating evidence in order to make judgements about whether practice is 'good' or 'good enough', if it is to become integral to the development of professional standards, then practitioners and users must begin to participate in its development and use. If they do not, then a great opportunity for evaluating practice will surely be lost.

In the final section of this chapter, a case example is presented of performance measurement in a probation service. This illustrates many of the issues raised in this chapter.

Case example

In one probation service, progress towards achieving the objectives of the agency's corporate strategy was monitored using a mosaic of methods: corporate strategy monitoring, principal customer satisfaction survey and area profiles. The monitoring exercise, undertaken at six-monthly intervals to identify progress or lack of progress in achieving the objectives of the corporate strategy, is illustrated below.

1. *Remands in custody*
   Targets were devised by the management team in light of data and interpretations from the previous year's information systems. Over the previous six months:
   % remands in custody: 6.1% (N = 643).
   Target set to reduce the remands in custody by 0.6%.
   Progress after three months: remands in custody: 6.9% (N = 360).
   Thus, no progress was made towards the target change: remands increased by 0.8%, a shortfall of 72 cases.
2. *Community supervision I*
   The objective for the next year is to be able to demonstrate that 80% of the community sentence orders supervised by the Service were successfully completed without further convictions.
   Previous six months: successful completions not

reconvicted 76.8% (N = 1,027); unsuccessful completions reconvicted 23.2% (N = 310).

Target set to change 3.2% (N = 43) of these unsuccessful orders to successes.

Subsequent six months: successful completions not reconvicted 73.3% (N = 475); unsuccessful completions reconvicted 26.7% (N = 173).

Thus, no progress was made towards the target change of 3.2% (N = 43): unsuccessful completions/reconvicted cases increased by 3.5% (N = 43), a shortfall of 43 cases.

3. *Community supervision II*

The objective for the next twelve months is to have provided improved equality of access to probation programmes by demonstrating that 50% of all new probation orders have an additional requirement for offenders convicted of the maximum band of 'serious enough' (for a community sentence) and 'so serious' (that custody is the only suitable sentence) offences. The additional requirements include: probation centre, young adult offender project, alcohol impaired drivers course, motor project, approved probation hostel.

Previous six months: probation orders with requirements in the top seriousness bands: 40% (N = 32); probation orders without requirements in the top seriousness bands: 60% (N = 48).

Target set to change 10% of latter to orders with requirements (N = 8).

Subsequent six months: the target change of 10% was exceeded by 7.7%; 14 additional orders with requirements were made in the top seriousness band.

4. *Equal opportunities*

The objective in the next year is to be able to demonstrate that 66% of Asians and 60% of African-Caribbeans on whom the service prepared pre-sentence reports (PSR) received a community sentence.

Previous six months: Asian offenders with PSRs given community sentences 59.5% (N = 44); Asian offenders with PSRs given custodial sentences 40.5% (N = 30).

Target set to change 6.5% (N = 5) of above custodial sentences to community sentences.

Subsequent six months: Asian offenders with PSRs given community sentences 79.2% (N = 57); Asian offenders with PSRs given custodial sentences 20.8% (N = 15). Thus, the target change of 6.5% was exceeded by 13.2%: total changes of 14 cases instead of 5.
Previous six months: African-Caribbean offenders with PSRs given community sentences 59.2% (N = 29); African-Caribbean offenders with PSRs given custodial sentences 40.8% (N = 20).
Target set to change these custodial sentences to community sentences by 0.8% (N = 1).
Subsequent six months: African-Caribbean offenders with PSRs given community sentences 60.9% (N = 39); African-Caribbean offenders with PSRs given custodial sentences 39.1% (N = 25).
Thus, the target change was exceeded by 0.9% (N = 1).

Note: In relation to the third, fourth and fifth targets, the figures are so small that a change of even one case would make a noticeable percentage difference.

This monitoring exercise illustrates several issues identified in this chapter.

- First, comparative data can be an important way to generate evidence. Comparisons made between different periods of time, and between different client groups and service responses can be useful.
- Second, data need to be selective, timely and parsimonious; it appears that these were in this example. However, the only guarantee of this is that they are clearly related to the service's objectives and owned by everyone in the agency.
- Third, the importance of change is illustrated. Data are not collected for their own sake but as an aid to development in relation to the agency's strategic objectives.

Data should be used as tin-openers rather than as dials. In other words, they are suggestive and provocative rather than explanatory, especially where numbers are small. Facts do not speak for themselves. Further analysis is required. For example, when progress is made towards the target change, possible reasons for this still need to be explored:

- Has the input of offenders changed in terms of their age, ethnicity, levels of social need?
- Has the throughput, in terms of probation officers' practices, changed: more imaginative and risk-taking assessments of non-custodial disposals; more thorough assessments: increased liaison with officers offering alternative disposals; developments in anti-discrimination practices?

Such evidence does not produce answers about the value of the service or practice, but rather it may be useful to inform processes of judgement-making about effectiveness. Did the changes indicate 'good' practices? Were Asian and African-Caribbean offenders given adequate and appropriate support in the community?

Similar issues need to be addressed when progress is not made in respect of targets:

- failure to reduce remands in custody may be because of lack of bail facilities, over-loaded probation officers, changes in patterns of offending, the practices of court officers, etc.;
- lack of progress in respect of reconvicted offenders on community supervision may relate to factors beyond the control of the probation service and its officers; levels of unemployment; police practices; offending opportunities; crime reduction policies.

The monitoring exercise attests to the importance and usefulness of baseline monitoring data collected over time in addressing progress made towards implementing a service's strategic objectives. However, they do not preclude the importance of debate about effectiveness, rather they inform it. Probation officers, with users and others having an interest in the service, have or may acquire the appropriate knowledge and skills to ask the kind of questions suggested above, to explore possible explanations, and to initiate appropriate changes. Such debate should be conducted adhering to the values and ethics underlying the criminal justice system and the probation service in a democratic society.

Mosaic of indicators

Performance measurement preferably should include a mosaic of data sources. In addition to the monitoring exercise, the same probation service undertook two further studies. First, it carried out a customer satisfaction survey of crown court judges focusing on pre-sentence reports, sentencing options, probation presence in court, post-sentence feedback.

The survey results revealed high overall levels of satisfaction. Areas highlighted for comment related to the boundaries between the probation service and the judiciary. For example, it was thought that officers underestimated the seriousness of offences and sometimes made unsuitable proposals; quality of supervision was seen to be more satisfactory than proposals for probation orders without conditions. Changes to improve feedback were recommended – for example, reviewing the liaison systems and appending original pre-sentence reports to progress reports. Probation officers' presence in court scored highest, with the exception of their clothing and punctuality.

Soft data can very usefully complement harder data in a mosaic. Judges' expressions of dissatisfaction do not necessarily indicate poor practices: they may also locate the boundaries of permitted and required practices which are legitimated by both legislation and the probation service's national and local statements of standards. If judges and probation officers always agreed about their assessments of seriousness and the suitability of proposals, the criminal justice system may not be functioning effectively (Hardiker, 1979).

The evidence generated through the survey suggests 'good' practice, especially in respect of some of the classical objectives of the probation service: quality and range of supervision and meeting the needs of the offender. It is important, though, to treat the evidence not as *the* truth, but as *a* truth that may inform processes of judgement-making about the effectiveness of practice. The reservations regarding the suitability of probation orders without requirements may indicate that there is further scope to increase the with-requirements option. Alternatively, it could again reflect a boundary issue in respect of the probation service and the judiciary; it may be appropriate for probation officers to propose a less-intrusive disposal even if the judiciary prefer to use more controlling sentencing options. Evaluation requires continuing questioning: for example, how are probation officers demarcating their professional and agency boundaries? Too much satisfaction may indicate that they are paying 'too much' attention to court requirements and 'too little' to their clients on supervision. Evaluating for 'good' practice must always question taken-for-granted assumptions and observations.

The probation service added further to the mosaic by using the Home Office Inspectorate of Probation area profile. This profile compares a service with similar 'baskets' of services using a range of statistical indicators: demographic, resources, staffing, costs and caseload activities. The work of the service is also summarised comparatively over a five-year time period. Again, the data are best used as a tin-opener rather than a dial to identify and then explore salient points and comparisons. For example, this service was seen to use community service orders less than others in similar situations. On further exploration there were good reasons for this discrepancy: more use was made of attendance centres.

The service also produced a corporate strategy and three-year plans, providing a framework and identifying service priorities. This strategy was then formulated in terms of aims, strategic statements and implementation procedures in respect of each stage of offence and offender careers. These included anticipated shortfalls and implementation gaps. A mosaic of performance measures was identified as a means of monitoring progress.

In conclusion

Presenting developments in performance measurement in one probation service has illustrated some of the ways in which data must be scrutinised further as evidence to inform judgements about practice. These exercises need not be implemented top-down and need not usurp agency objectives by being too data-driven. Probation officers, individually and in their teams, could ask the kind of evaluation questions outlined. Their values, knowledge and skills should enable them to extend such questioning to others, such as their clients, and to debate reasons why progress is or is not being made towards achieving strategic objectives. This may also indicate ways in which they are exploiting the structural space available to them and appropriately demarcating the boundaries of their professionalism.

5

Towards a Critical Approach to Evaluation

So far we have focused our writing on rational-technical approaches to evaluation because, to a significant extent, they have become synonymous with evaluation. Also, in our experience, it is these forms of evaluation that most alienate practitioners and encourage (rightly in our view) suspicion about the values and purposes of evaluation.

In the previous chapter, we alerted practitioners to ways in which quantitative measures of performance may be used technically as 'dials'. In the market economy of social welfare, such a rational-technical approach to performance measurement, underpinned by the notion of causality relating input and output, is being applied to such an extent that a form of managerial evaluation is emerging. Evaluation thus is rapidly becoming part of the repertoire of those controlling policy and resource allocation mechanisms.

In making this argument we are not rejecting the quantitative measurement of indicators of performance. Indicators can, if used as 'tin-openers', prompt projects and organisations into raising questions about their practice, a practice which otherwise might be taken-for-granted and assumed to be 'good'. For example, our discussion of performance indictors in the probation service showed how data may be interrogated to suggest contrasting explanations. In searching for an evaluation approach that may go some way towards meeting the conditions we have set for ourselves, we find it useful to look beyond positivism into alternative social science paradigms of interpretivism and critical theory. Postmodernist understandings of power and knowledge, and their interrelationship, help us to comprehend our concerns about rational-technical evaluation, or managerial evaluation. They also guide us into evaluation approaches that have the possibility of facilitating the movement of practice in the direction of the 'good'.

In this chapter, we now explore evaluation approaches located within these alternative paradigms, acknowledging the significance of subjectivity, values and power in the shaping of understandings of programmes, projects and practice. We interrogate these ways of evaluating for their possible contribution towards the development of 'good' or 'good enough' practice. We reach conclusions about a critical approach to evaluation informed by postmodernist understandings and, in the chapters that follow, consider ways in which to implement such an approach.

Critical evaluators

The evaluation literature of the last thirty years, in the USA and the UK, abounds both with criticisms of rational-technical approaches and with worked-out alternatives. By the 1960s, in the USA particularly, evaluators were confronted with a host of well-founded criticisms. Indeed, Weiss comments that

> it sometimes seems that more papers have been published criticising evaluation practices and procedures than reporting the results of studies conducted. (Weiss, 1986b: 145)

Those working in the voluntary and statutory sectors are often expected to produce output and outcome measures of their practice as though these measures themselves produce proof of value, as 'dials' rather than 'tin-openers'. Amongst evaluators, however, there has been long and continuing debate about more appropriate ways in which to evaluate effectiveness. Knowing that there are alternatives should alert us to possible political motives behind today's managerial initiatives introduced supposedly to assure quality in service.

Evaluators have been concerned to address criticisms of them as:

- posing as neutral, objective 'scientific experts' and thus masking and not acknowledging, or allowing to be publicly acknowledged, their own values;
- being top-down, outside-in controllers of information, not learning from developmental practices;
- acting in cosy relationships with their 'clients', funders, sponsors and managers;
- context-stripping, blaming the victims, e.g. grass-roots practitioners of ill-managed and/or resourced social welfare programmes and projects that fail to provide evidence of effectiveness against pre-determined objectives and criteria for measurement;
- failing to influence practice and policy change and development through their lack of attention to making evaluations usable, and to utilisation of their findings.

Smith and Cantley describe rational-technical approaches to evaluation as 'generally favouring senior management and other "top dogs"' (Smith and Cantley, 1985: 5). They point to the powerful effect of the interrelationship between, on the one hand, rational-technical approaches to both evaluation and the policy process and, on the other, an approach that regards organisations as in consensus rather than as places in which different interests and values are played out. Such a

> rationalistic approach is too narrow in neglecting a range of significant political variables, especially the power of relevant vested interests. (Smith and Cantley, 1985: 5)

Interpretivist evaluations

The first responses to the criticisms of rational-technical evaluations came from evaluators approaching understandings of the world within an interpretivist, sometimes called naturalistic, paradigm. Within this paradigm a number of slightly different versions of what may be regarded as interpretivist evaluations have developed: for example, formative evaluation; illuminative evaluation (e.g. Parlett and Hamilton, 1976); stakeholder evaluation (Guba and Lincoln, 1981; Gold, 1981); user studies (Rees and Wallace, 1982); pluralist evaluation (Smith and Cantley, 1985); fourth generation evaluation (Guba and Lincoln, 1989). Each version tends to emphasise different aspects of evaluation, some focusing more on the relationship between evaluation and policy and practice change, others highlighting the diverse interests of people involved in the practice being evaluated. We briefly describe some of these different versions below. Our intention is both to open up access to these alternative approaches and to interrogate them for their ability to meet the conditions we have set for effective evaluation.

While there are some significant differences between these approaches, they all assume that the social world is fundamentally different from the physical and natural one in that it is made up of people with subjectivities. Subjectivity cannot be eliminated by controlling it. To pretend to such an endeavour is to fail to capture the richness and variety of people's subjective understandings. And to assert that values can be eliminated through control is to negate the inevitable influence of values on data collected and on their analysis: thus leaving such values intact and implicit. This applies to the subjectivities and values of all involved in the evaluation process. So, rather than knowledge of practices and programmes being generated through supposedly neutral and objective data collection and analysis processes, these are treated as being given meaning by the range of actors involved in the practice. It is these meanings that are sought by the evaluator. This position is clearly articulated by Smith and Cantley, for example, in proposing

> the need to develop a more pluralistic approach which could cope with diversity and conflict. A more subjectivist methodology would promote the collection of multiple perspectives on the programme (not necessarily in agreement with each other) and would incorporate them into the evaluation exercise. Ambiguity and lack of agreement in perception between parties of the policy-shaping community would then be a central feature of the research, rather than an embarrassment as is the case when the presumption of consensus fails. (Smith and Cantley, 1985: 8–9)

These evaluations, then, reject the notion of value-free, neutral objectivity. Instead, evaluation:

- seeks to capture people's understandings of what is going on and to what effect, recognising that these will not be the same for all people;
- reflects on the subjectivity of the evaluator, recognised as important to the development of understanding;
- focuses on processes through which meanings are attached to practices and programmes;
- reveals understandings rather than causal explanations;
- tends to generate qualitative data and analyses these as such;
- focuses on meanings ascribed by people;
- does not control or pretend to eliminate values but treats them as fundamental to the meanings people attach to their experiences.

Having regard to equality, this approach is clearly an advance on the managerial, rational-technical model in that it accords all involved, including users, the right to know and be heard. And the evaluators must make their own subjective values explicit. The approach holds evaluators accountable for their values.

Formative and summative evaluation

Evaluations within an interpretivist paradigm place emphasis on process instead of, or as well as, product. The focus is upon generating understandings of the meaning of practice rather than on measuring its effects by determining cause-and-effect relationships. Sometimes in the literature these different approaches are referred to as formative (process) as distinct from summative (product) evaluations. Reith (1984) distinguishes 'formative' as focusing on process, often regarded as action-research, and 'summative' as focusing on outcomes.

Illuminative evaluation

Evaluators of educational programmes have developed what they term 'illuminative evaluation' (Parlett and Hamilton, 1972; Buist, 1984). The primary task of this evaluative approach is to illuminate, to shed light upon, what is going on in the practice. It focuses on the processes of practice and seeks to provide a 'description and interpretation in context' (Buist, 1984: 94).

Gordon (1991) adopts an illuminative evaluation approach for evaluating and improving social work practice. He describes illuminative evaluation as

> helping people understand the most significant aspects of an entire milieu, including important structures and interrelationships, negotiations between parties, reciprocal influences, alternative conceptualisations and value orientations, critical processes, resource utilisation, and any other aspects of the environment deemed significant. The milieu is viewed

as a transactional field in which actors are inseparable from their setting. (Gordon, 1991: 371)

There is a lot to unpack here. Gordon points out that illuminative evaluation does not only focus on process but also takes account of the relationships between structural and interpersonal factors in practice. The emphasis is on evaluating practice in context. The approach recognises that practice comprises a set of actors who may have very different values and expectations. Furthermore any practice involves negotiating these differences. This approach to illuminative evaluation brings us to the work of evaluators who have placed emphasis on these actors, or 'stakeholders' as they have been termed.

Actors and stakeholders

Two important features are now emerging in our setting out of the evaluation debate from an interpretivist perspective. First, evaluation is about understanding what goes on in practice, i.e. making the implicit explicit. It seeks to answer the question, what are the meanings and interpretations of practice held by those involved in it? Second, practice comprises sets of processes which are continuously negotiated by the actors involved, each having different interests, values and expectations of practice. This has led evaluators to pay attention to these different actors, to their subjectivities, particularly recognising that these actors have varying interests, or stakes, in the practice. We have now moved quite a way from evaluation being undertaken by an external expert and treating practice as an entity to be measured objectively, separated from its context and from those constructing it.

Evaluators have argued for a stakeholder approach on epistemological, political and utilisation grounds. Epistemologically the case is made for generating evidence of practice by exploring the range of understandings, expectations and experiences of practice on the part of those involved in it: funders, policy-makers, managers, workers, volunteers, users, referral agents, etc. Politically, this approach to evaluation enhances people's participation in making judgements about whether the practice is 'good', 'good enough' or 'poor'. And thirdly, the argument is made that, if people having an interest in the practice are involved in its evaluation, then they are much more likely to be receptive to the findings and recommendations for change that emerge through the evaluation process. As Weiss remarks about stakeholder evaluation:

> There is a delicious flavour to the concept. It tackles some of the pervasive problems that have plagued evaluation, and it addresses them with high-minded intent and plausible strategies of action. (Weiss, 1986b: 151)

However, Weiss continues by pointing out complexities in the approach. The first concerns difficulties in deciding who are the stakeholders to be involved in the evaluation. Some define stakeholders as those who have responsibility to make decisions about the future of the practice, programme or project that is being evaluated. Others define stakeholders more broadly as 'all the people whose lives are affected by the program and its evaluation' (Weiss, 1986b: 151).

Case example

The following were included in the evaluation of the arts programme in elderly persons' homes on the grounds that they all should participate in judgement-making about the project:

- older people resident in the homes or attending the day centre who participated in the sessions;
- older people resident in the homes or attending the

day centre who did not participate in the sessions;

- care assistants in the residential homes and the day centre involved in the project;
- those with management responsibilities in the homes and the day centre;
- those with management and/or training responsibilities in the Social Services Department and the Arts & Libraries Department;
- those with management and/or training responsibilities at the voluntary agency;
- the arts workers;
- others who may have participated but did not include relatives and friends of the older people, GPs and other professionals working with the older people, members of the management committee of the voluntary agency responsible for the project, the funders from statutory and charitable sources and so on.

(Everitt, 1994)

The list of possible stakeholders is endless. Deciding where to draw the line as to who should be involved as stakeholders would be the first task in designing such an evaluation. Deciding who should have a say in judging effectiveness is critical to the outcomes of the evaluation. Guba and Lincoln (1981) identify three broad groups of stakeholders:

- agents: those responsible for providing the service, running the project, implementing the programme, such as funders, managers, workers, members of management committees;
- beneficiaries: those who are meant to benefit directly or indirectly from the project, programme or practice;
- victims: those who would be expected to be affected negatively if the project is successful, such as, for example, sexual harassers and abusers through the work of a project dealing with sexual violence, white middle-

class women through a new opportunities for women project targeted at women, black and white, most likely to be excluded from education and training.

If it is the evaluator who decides on who to include as a stakeholder then we may yet again be assigning the evaluator with too much power. Certainly in stakeholder evaluation the evaluator becomes negotiator and educator with expertise in ways to generate evidence:

> The stakeholder approach changes the role of evaluators. They are asked not only to be technical experts who do competent research. They are required to become political managers who orchestrate the involvement of diverse groups. They must be negotiators, weighing one set of information requests against others and coming to amicable agreements about priorities. They must be skilful educators, sharing their knowledge about appropriate expectations for program development and program success while giving participants a sense of ownership of the study. (Weiss, 1986b: 153)

Pluralist evaluation

Smith and Cantley (1985) employed a stakeholder model in their evaluation of a psychogeriatric day hospital. They named their approach to evaluation 'pluralist', emphasising the plurality of perspectives in any evaluation involving a wide range of participants that then need to be taken into account. In their study, stakeholders were asked for accounts of the parts they played in the provision and development of services provided through the day hospital. Furthermore, they were asked to reflect on ways in which they determined whether the services were effective or not. Smith and Cantley write:

> We have termed our approach 'pluralistic' evaluation'. The central point we are making is that if we are to understand

> and evaluate the part played by the several different groups involved in the care of a client group then we must understand how they use different criteria of success in their own interests and how 'success' thus operates in the social context of its use. (Smith and Cantley, 1985: 12)

They attribute their thinking to theories of political pluralism, to incrementalist approaches to the policy process and to the

> 'subjectivist' tradition of research within sociology which takes the actors' 'definition of the situation' as a starting-point for investigation. (Smith and Cantley, 1985: 12)

They outline the stages in the design of their pluralist evaluation thus:

- identification of stakeholders and comparison of their perspectives and practices;
- collection of data about these perspectives and practices as they inform the ways in which the stakeholders view success;
- recording of plurality of ideas of success and the practices implemented by stakeholders to achieve success as defined in their own terms;
- assessment of the extent to which success in its varying definitions is achieved or not;
- employment of a broad range of data collection methods recognising that using a single method may favour some stakeholders over others;
- the creation of qualitative accounts of the ways in which the services have developed together with more explanatory reasons for them having developed in these ways.

Smith and Cantley (1985) defend their approach from criticisms of bias precisely because they do take into account the fact that different people involved in practice, in a project or programme, will have different interests and will pursue these interests in the course of their involvement:

> While pluralistic evaluation may seem complex and uncertain in its use of multiple criteria, it cannot be dismissed for failure to take at least some account of the perspective of any significant group of participants. While most 'objective' evaluation seeks to remain politically neutral but in practice becomes hopelessly embroiled in the politics of the organisation being studied (even if the evaluators do not always realise what is happening), pluralistic evaluation stands some chance of remaining 'independent' and 'neutral' by having taken sympathetic account of as many perspectives as possible. By taking the political processes of the agency seriously there is some chance that the political role of evaluation itself will be clarified. (Smith and Cantley, 1985: 14)

The debate has now moved on somewhat. We now see acknowledged in the literature and amongst evaluators that evaluation is about:

- revealing what goes on in practice while recognising that practice is not a discrete external objective reality separate from those involved in it but is constructed through the meanings and interpretations they attach to it;
- acknowledging that practice comprises sets of processes which are continuously negotiated by all those involved, each having different interests, values and expectations of practice;
- being aware that people's interests in practice, which they pursue through their contributions to practice and to its evaluation, constitute political interests and thus may be conceptualised in terms of who loses and who gains.

We turn now to the last of the approaches that falls within an interpretivist paradigm while straddling somewhat the critical paradigm by taking account of power, albeit to a limited extent.

Fourth-generation evaluation

Having ascertained the perspectives and criteria of success of stakeholders, the problem that Smith and Cantley (1985) are left with is how to judge between different views. Is it enough for the evaluator or the evaluation process to leave this to the plurality of interests represented in the policy arena and to the workings out of competing interests through incremental processes? Our approach to evaluation, that of making judgements about 'good' or 'good enough' or 'poor' or even 'corrupt' practice does not absolve the evaluation from this responsibility. It is, after all, the purpose of evaluation.

Guba and Lincoln (1989) take us slightly further in focusing upon the processes through which different views are articulated and debated. They assume that it is the responsibility of the evaluation to ensure that different views of participants in the practice, project or programme are not only expressed but are also heard by each other. The evaluator's task is to facilitate this process, to enable those with different perspectives to communicate these to each other, to generate debate about practice and provide evidence that will help inform disagreements and bring about resolution.

> one of the major tasks of the evaluator is to conduct the evaluation in such a way that each group must confront and deal with the constructions of all the others, a process we shall refer to as a hermeneutic dialectic. In that process some, perhaps many, of the original claims, concerns, and issues may be settled without recourse to new information, that is,

> information that is not already available from one or more of the stakeholding groups themselves. As each group copes with the constructions posed by others, their own constructions alter by virtue of becoming better informed and more sophisticated. Ideally, responsive evaluation seeks to reach consensus on all claims, concerns, and issues at this point, but that is rarely if ever possible. Conflicts remain whose resolution requires the introduction of outside information, which it becomes the evaluator's task to obtain. (Guba and Lincoln, 1989: 41)

The final conclusions and recommendations arising from the evaluation are 'arrived at jointly; they are never the unique or sole province of the evaluator or client' (Guba and Lincoln, 1989: 42). Furthermore, Guba and Lincoln recognise that such agreed conclusions may never be reached but at least the stakeholders will admit conflicts between them and realise where each of them stands in relation to disagreements. The answer here, for Guba and Lincoln, is to appreciate that evaluation is never finished, never complete. It may come to interim conclusions but there will usually be more concerns and issues to evaluate over which there is seeming disagreement and conflict in the project or organisation. Evaluation thus becomes not so much an activity at one stage in the life of a project or programme but a continuing process concerned with generating evidence to inform debate between interested parties.

One of the difficulties for evaluation within an interpretivist paradigm is to respond to the criticism that seeking out and listening to everyone's subjective experience and interpretation of the practice may lead to a relativist 'anything goes' position. Do the stakeholders of projects have equal rights to be heard? Does every view count equally? Guba and Lincoln's response to this criticism is to place trust in the process, to have regard for the potential of people to listen to and be informed by each other and to be responsive to evidence. The role of the evaluator is to facilitate this process and, perhaps with more radical potential:

> The moral imperative . . . is continuously to be on the alert for – indeed, to seek out – challenges to the prevailing construction (however much it may be supported in consensus), and to stand ready to refine, change, or even reject that which is currently believed in favour of something else that, on examination, seems more reasonable and appropriate to those in the best position to make that judgement. (Guba and Lincoln, 1989: 47)

Here critical elements are entering the evaluation debate which we think bring us nearer to an approach which has a chance of meeting the conditions we have set for ourselves. The evaluator, as well as acting in roles as researcher, negotiator and educator, is assigned moral responsibility. And this responsibility is to do with being critical of the status quo, facilitating groups not only where there is observable conflict but where a consensus can mask dimensions of power and powerlessness. As Lukes asks:

> is it not the supreme exercise of power to get another or others to have the desires you want them to have – that is, to secure their compliance by controlling their thoughts and desires? (Lukes, 1974: 23)

Paraphrasing the words of Guba and Lincoln, the question is how does evaluation reach conclusions about what 'seems more reasonable and appropriate' than the prevailing consensus and status quo and who are the people 'in the best position to make that judgement'(1989: 47)? For us, the answers are best found in critical social science and postmodern paradigms that turn the attention of researchers and evaluators to power and the powerful processes through which subjectivities are constructed.

Towards a critical evaluation

Critical theorists criticise interpretivists for their failure to take account of the structures and processes through which subjectivities are shaped and maintained. There are theories of power which help locate people's views of their experiences and their expectations of, and aspirations for, social welfare projects and programmes. These theories, too, help to decide who to include on the list of stakeholders and, furthermore, to actively draw into the process those who otherwise might be excluded. In informing and facilitating the evaluation process, theories of power help to understand whose interests may be actively articulated, by themselves and others, at the expense of whom. Structural and interpersonal expressions of power render some as powerful and others as powerless. It is these forms of power that can provoke both conflict and consensus in the project or organisation. If evaluation is to be effective in ensuring 'good' practice and revealing or inhibiting 'poor' and 'corrupt' practice, it needs to develop ways to puncture consensuses that produce taken-for-granted, uncontested ways of understanding and intervention that may not be in everyone's interests.

Critical social science can help in a number of ways in our search for such an evaluation model. It:

- locates social welfare projects, programmes and practices, and people's understandings and evaluations of them, historically and in their social, political and economic contexts;
- reveals how dimensions of oppression such as social class, gender, race, age, disability and sexuality generate and maintain certain practices and understandings;
- deconstructs commonly accepted ways of doing things

and understandings so that these are not taken-for-granted but are exposed for the extent to which they both influence and are influenced by prevailing ways of thinking;

- is informed by theories of democracy and social justice that help to guide both the processes of judgement-making and the judgements to be made;
- is committed to provoking change in the direction of equality.

Thus, evaluation within a critical social science paradigm will be concerned to:

- capture people's understandings of what the project does and with what effects, recognising that these will not be the same for all people;
- theorise people's understandings, and differences between people's understandings, by locating these in relation to social class, gender, race, age, disability, and sexuality;
- be a dialogical process, a process of emancipatory reasoning, focusing on oppressive mechanisms that influence the understandings of all involved;
- develop as a process that encompasses strategies for policy and change, revealed as necessary through the evaluation;
- reveal understandings as well as quasi-causal explanations;
- generate both qualitative or quantitative data and analyse them as such;
- not control or pretend to eliminate values, but regard them as fundamental and therefore to be made explicit and challenged.

The evaluation process may be conceptualised in two phases although in practice these are interrelated. First is the phase of generating evidence about the practice, the programme or project. Critical social science theorises the ways in which people's views, experiences, aspirations and expectations are shaped through dimensions such as age, class, gender, race, sexuality and disability. Through their understanding of the ideological shaping of subjectivities, critical social scientists claim that they are able to generate a more true version of reality than interpretivists who accept subjectivity at face value. Rather than generate ideologically constructed versions of reality, through their methods of data collection and analysis, critical social scientists claim that they can take account of ideology in their search for truth.

The second interrelated phase of evaluation is that of making judgements about whether the practice is 'good', 'good enough' or 'poor' or 'corrupt'. Critical social science provides us with standards against which to make such judgements: standards of justice and equality.

Case example

The evaluation of the young women's project based in an area of social and economic disadvantage did not only involve stakeholders who could readily be identified as being associated with the project. Certainly, there were such people who were involved in the evaluation from the beginning: the workers in the project; the local authority personnel who were responsible for recommending to the authority that it continue to grant-aid the project; members of the voluntary management committee, there as professionals, feminists and/or former and current users; volunteers; and workers in other agencies such as a nearby family centre and the area office of the social services department which refer young women to the project. The project's aims included a commitment to making the project accessible to all young women, Black and white. The evaluation adopted this commitment as a statement of equality and justice by which the work of the project could be evaluated.

Generating evidence about the project revealed that the meaning of this commitment was becoming increasingly contested as the project employed Black workers with different views about the needs of young Black women. Some workers, Black and white, felt that it was alright that Black young women did not use the project. They argued that the project was not appropriate for young Black women who would be better served by developing their own activities like sewing groups. The project currently offered discussion groups and activities that would facilitate discussion around issues such as single parenting, child abuse, and domestic violence. Other workers, Black and white, argued strongly that the project and all of its activities should be more accessible to Black young women. Additionally there should be some Black-only groups to provide space for Black women to share accounts of their experiences and develop understandings of racism.

Taking a critical social science perspective, the evaluation did not accept all the workers' views at face value, a process which would have resulted in a plurality of perspectives being documented. It theorised race and racism as influencing the views of white and Black workers. It engaged in a process of data generation and debate in the project to address more critically the processes that resulted both in the de-politicising of the lives of young Black women and in leaving invisible to the project young Black women living in the locality. The evaluation team was expanded to include a Black woman and data were collected to identify potential stakeholders, potential users. The picture that emerged was of a predominantly white locality with issues of racism being experienced directly by women of mixed ethnicities who sometimes identified themselves as white, sometimes as Black. There were also issues of racism for young white mothers with Black children.

The Black member of the evaluation team conducted a study day with the project to facilitate informed debate about race and ethnicity in the project. For debate, or critical dialogue, the project had before it the data that had been generated in such a way as to take account of race and racism. The study day also was concerned to develop some agreed priorities for the future work of the project. (Everitt and Johnson, 1992)

This analysis of evaluation approaches and their development across positivist, interpretivist and critical paradigms shows a continuing struggle on the part of evaluators to refine their methodologies and methods to generate the truths of the practice, programme or project. What is going on? What is being achieved? Is it 'good', 'good enough', 'poor' or 'corrupt'? Who thinks so and who doesn't? Who decides?

These are the difficult questions that have troubled evaluators. However, for us, those evaluators who take account of subjectivity and have an understanding of relationships between subjectivity and power are more likely to generate sensitive and political understandings of practice and its value. A critical approach to evaluation that recognises dimensions of power and treats evaluation, practice and the policy arena as political processes would seem to meet our conditions for effective evaluation.

At this stage it is useful to reflect back on those conditions to test the relevance of critical social science approaches:

- the importance of moral debate and everybody, irrespective of power, status and position, having the right to legitimate opinions.

Critical social science puts faith in what is called the process of emancipatory reasoning. Through reasoning and debate, the truth of practice and the extent to which it is moving in the direction of the 'good' would become evident.

- scepticism of rational-technical modes of practice.

Critical evaluators understand the rational-technical mode for the Ways in which, through supposed control of values, it fails to take them into account, leaving them unchallenged. It thus maintains the status quo and serves powerful interests.

- the recognition of power, powerlessness and empowerment.

Critical evaluators have an understanding of structural and interpersonal processes of power and engage in evaluation as a tool for empowerment, or, in other words, to achieve practice and policy change for equality.

- the development of genuine dialogue between users and those within the organisation, and within the organisation itself.

Critical evaluation engages with users in dialogical processes to provide opportunities for them to develop greater understandings, and through these, enhanced control of their lives. Consciousness-raising is valued as a process through which people lift the mantles of ideology to reveal their true experiences, feelings and views. Users of services within social welfare would be regarded as people likely to be discriminated against through dimensions of race, gender, disability, age and sexuality.

- attention to be paid to the fundamental purpose of the organisation and caution about becoming diverted into demonstrating productivity.

The critical evaluator would pay attention to the purpose of the organisation regarding this as a statement not only of goals and objectives but of values. This would be used by the critical evaluator to facilitate judgement-making about the programme, project or practice.

- the encouragement of openness, questioning, complaints and criticisms from outside and within the organisation.

Critical evaluation is about opening up the influence of

ideology. It questions what appears to be, scrutinising the taken-for-granted, ensuring that people are not saying about a service, policy, organisation what they think they are supposed to say. Evaluation within this paradigm would provide space so that people may feel free to be critical without fear of being penalised.

- the removal of 'otherness' that may be attributed to those lower in the hierarchy, to users and to those relatively powerless in the community.

Critical evaluators, having an awareness of power and powerful processes, would be alert to those who usually are excluded from meaningful decision-making about services, policies and their development. Critical evaluation would ensure that such people, particularly workers and users, have a say in judging the effectiveness of projects. It would ensure that people are not marginalised through racism and/or sexism or because of their social class, age, disabilities or sexual orientations.

We are still not sure however about claims that critical social scientists make to the effect that they are able to lift the mantle of ideology to discover the real views and experiences of people. This reliance on reasoning as a way of seeking out the truth does not fit with our experience of the ways in which such judgements are made in organisations. In our view, the social world of practice is such as to suggest that there are potentially many truths. There is no one answer. Processes of generating and debating evidence of practice in evaluation do not produce the truth of practice. They may produce an agreed version that will do for the moment. The processes of generating and scrutinising evidence do not obviate the need, in the end, to make moral judgements about whether practice is 'good', 'good enough', 'poor' or 'corrupt'.

The contribution of postmodernist theory to evaluation

Postmodernism shifts us into a completely different way of thinking about the process of getting to know about the social world. In the continual search for the truth, postmodernist thinkers, influenced for example by Foucault (for example, Weedon, 1987; Rojeck, Peacock and Collins, 1988; Fox, 1993), regard the task of the social scientist as one to do with digging around to reveal ways by which some things, some ways of thinking about the world, about people, about practice, come to be regarded as true. Rather than reveal truth (as positivists claim to do through their objective and neutral methodologies, as interpretivists claim by capturing real subjective experiences, as critical theorists claim by lifting the mystification of ideology from people's real views and experiences), postmodernists claim to reveal ways in which truth is produced.

For postmodernists, the claim to truth is inextricably linked with powerful processes. Science, and claims to be scientific, constitute for postmodernists a powerful enterprise through which the knowledge constructed by its methods comes to be thought of as truth. Positivist evaluation, or managerial evaluation, relying on measures of performance and causal relationships between inputs and outputs, may be so understood. A postmodernist evaluator, if there were such a person, would be alert to the ways in which positivist, rational-technical evaluation approaches coalesce with new managerialism to form a powerful discourse of managerial evaluation. Barrett, in her explanation of Foucault's approach, refers to his

> account of the role of 'disciplines' in the management of truth. . . . Disciplines operate with certain rules . . . science has become institutionalised as power, and the 'will to truth' is a key dimension of that historical process. (Barrett, 1991: 142–3)

Evaluation may be understood as one of these disciplines. Discourse in the sense used above relates to the idea of the 'discursive field' developed by Foucault to conceptualise:

> the relationship between language, social institutions, subjectivity and power. Discursive fields consist of competing ways of giving meaning to the world and of organising social institutions and processes. (Weedon, 1987: 35)

It is through discourses (comprising texts, languages, behaviours, a multitude of policies and practices) that both knowledge, what we know, and subjectivity, how we come to be known, are constructed. So, for example, the 'single parent' (imagine her!) is constructed through texts, the media, the talk of politicians, policies and social work practices as though it has some real and natural meaning independent of these. Discourses coalesce to form broader, more encompassing discursive fields, for example 'the family', which themselves give rise to more discourses. In that these discourses name the world for us, they in effect form powerful images of the truth: they operate in ways to effect the truth.

So, the term 'the politics of truth' is used to indicate that science, evaluation, conceptual analysis, and language, do not uncover the truth but contribute to its construction through the formation of discourses and discursive fields. Thus, for postmodernists, 'truth', while maybe an ideal in the quest for indisputable, universal knowledge, is always to be deconstructed for the ways in which it has arisen through these powerful processes.

A critical evaluation, then, informed by postmodernist theorising, suspends the process of seeking causal relationships between inputs and outputs, becoming more aware of 'the polymorphous cluster of correlations' that constitute discourses and discursive fields, 'regimes of truth' (Foucault, 1968: quoted by Barrett, 1991: 130). The programme, project and practices to be evaluated would be understood as being constructed through discourses, which in turn need to be understood in terms of power: whose interests do they serve? The task of evaluation is to contribute to the deconstruction of discourses that serve consistently to render some (for example, young women who are mothers; Black youth) less powerful than others.

Postmodernism has been heavily criticised as lapsing into total relativism. In other words, if there is no truth but rather many truths constructed through discourses, then in the end is there any way of knowing whether the practice is 'good', 'good enough', 'poor' or even 'corrupt'? Now with a model of evaluation that takes account of power and powerful processes, in our next chapter we analyse needs discourses in an attempt to show ways in which welfare policies and practices are politically contested. Then in Chapter 7 we attempt to suggest ways in which evidence of practice may be generated to inform judgement-making for the 'good'.

There is not one truth to be revealed but many truths and perspectives articulated, suppressed, negotiated, compromised through discourses, through processes of power and powerlessness. Such an epistemological position, rather than claiming the truth of the knowledge generated, allows for, indeed makes necessary, the need for moral decision-making and judgement-making. Judgements about the good are not self-evident truths derived from measuring cause and effect relations between input and outcomes. But nor can there, in the end, be a plurality of notions of what is 'good' and what is not. The process of judgement-making is the focus of Chapter 8.

6

Designs for Critical Evaluation

In this chapter, we draw upon the work of two postmodernist writers to outline frameworks that may be useful in designing that part of evaluation which is to do with generating evidence. The first, Layder (1993), sets out a research map. This clarifies different, but interrelated, levels of social life which impinge on, and are constructed through, activities, or practice. Second, Fraser's analysis of need (1989) illustrates ways in which discourses may be analysed. In the next chapter, using the postmodernist work of Fox (1993), we explore ways in which alternative discourses may be fostered. He provides ideas for alternative ways of approaching the eliciting of, and meaning of, user views. We illustrate the chapter with examples drawn from our own attempts to evaluate for 'good' practice.

A resource map for generating evidence

Layder (1993) develops a research strategy to cut through the objectivity/subjectivity dichotomy pursued by both positivists and interpretivists. He is concerned to bring together the analysis of the macro and micro, the social structural and the personal, understanding ways in which these are interdependent. As he says,

> it is best to understand macro and micro features as intermingling with each other through the medium of social activity. (Layder, 1993: 71)

In other words, it is through researching the practices of an organisation or programme that evidence is generated of both micro and macro features. This evidence may illuminate the ways in which practices, or activities, maintain and reproduce power relations, say gender inequality (a macro, social structural dimension). At the same time, the data may reveal, at a micro level, ways in which interpersonal interactions, say between men and women in the organisation, display and form gendered power relations. Furthermore, the personal experiences, understandings and feelings of women workers, with respect to, say, their marginalisation, may also be uncovered. The analysis is not one that demonstrates causal, deterministic relations between the social structural dimension of gender on the one hand and women's marginalisation on the other. Rather, practices coalesce to form discourses through which women workers come to be regarded, and to regard themselves, in particular ways so effecting gender inequality, patterned and pervasive to such an extent that it may be understood as structural. Layder sets out this kind of analysis of the intermingling of macro and micro thus:

> macro phenomena make no sense unless they are related to the social activities of individuals who reproduce them over time. Conversely, micro phenomena cannot be fully understood by exclusive reference to their 'internal dynamics', so to speak, they have to be seen to be conditioned by circumstances inherited from the past. In other words, micro phenomena have to be understood in relation to the influence of the institutions that provide their wider social context. In this respect macro and micro phenomena are inextricably bound together through the medium of social activity. (Layder, 1993: 102–3)

To develop a practical schema of this conceptualising of the research task, Layder constructs what he calls 'a resource map for research'. This portrays the different levels of social life, each 'closely interrelated, but which for analytic and research purposes can be scrutinized separately' (Layder, 1993: 71). This research map is set out here:

Research Map

Research Element	Research focus
Context	Values, traditions, social and power relations such as class, gender, race relations
Setting	Immediate environment of social activity such as school, family, team, project, community group
Situated activity	Interpersonal relations and the dynamics of face-to-face interaction, focusing on emergent meanings as these are affected by context, setting and individuals
Self	Biographical experience and social involvements as influenced by and interacting with the above

HISTORY (↕)

(Adapted from Layder, 1993)

Layder stresses the textured and interwoven nature of these different levels and dimensions of social reality which represent a continuous process unfolding over time. Power is central to this map of a stratified society.

The map is best used to help plan and design research (or evaluation) projects. It serves as a reminder of the complexity of layers of any project or programme to be evaluated. It may act as a 'prompt' or 'sounding board' 'that may provide new "lines of attack" or fresh angles on the problem, issue or topic at hand' (Layder, 1993: 73).

Case example

In designing an evaluation of the arts project with older people living in local authority residential homes, reference to the map (and this is adapted from Layder 1993: 71–106) suggests that evidence of practice be generated to answer, for example, the following questions:

In relation to the self and situated activity: What residents' subjective feelings are associated with the arts activities, feelings such as entrapment, fulfilment, contentment, elation, independence, self-esteem, attitudes to authority?

In relation to situated activity: Who is doing what to whom in the arts activities? What forms of communication are being used, verbal and non-verbal, and are they accessible to everyone? Who, if anybody, is marginalised?

In relation to social setting: What forms of power, authority and control are there in the home, between staff (officers, care workers, arts workers and residents, men and women)? What resources underpin these? To what extent does conflict and tension characterise the setting, overt or covert? How are these resolved, if at all? What difference does the introduction of the arts make, if any?

In relation to context: What general distribution of power and resources in society is relevant to the analysis of these practices in the homes: e.g. gender relations and participation in the arts by men and women residents; gender and class relations and the working conditions of care assistants? What values, ideas and ideologies encourage or discourage certain forms of behaviour on the part of women care assistants and residents, men and women?

Furthermore, a historical dimension to the questioning and analysis will provide evidence of how the different levels change over time and how power relations have emerged historically:

> A historical dimension reveals that the way in which people live out their lives on a daily basis (that is, the routine interweaving of identities, interactions, settings and contexts) is intimately associated with the long-term evolution of institutions forms of power. (Layder, 1993: 208–9)

In terms of evaluation, focus on the different levels of analysis of social life and on historical, social and political processes requires a multi-faceted research strategy. On the one hand, this should avoid taking social structures as given and deterministic. On the other, it does not treat individual subjective expressions of experience as truth, an interpretivist approach which results in a relativist, anything goes stance. Rather, practice is approached as the interdependence of interpersonal and the more structural dimensions of social life. For a critical evaluation, then, evidence of practice is generated by exploring different levels of social life and the ways in which these are negotiated historically through powerful social relations.

Analysing discourses

Needs are central to contemporary welfare discourses and key to evaluating whether a project or programme is effective. As such, Fraser's (1989) analysis of discourses of needs provides a valuable framework for the design of critical evaluations. We illustrate her analysis with 'needs discourses' drawn from three social services contexts. Fraser takes as her starting point Foucault's view (1979), that

> need is . . . a political instrument, meticulously prepared, calculated and used. (Foucault, 1979: 26)

As Fraser argues,

> needs talk functions as a medium for the making and contesting of political claims . . . It is an idiom in which political conflict is played out and through which inequalities are symbolically elaborated and challenged . . . in welfare state societies, needs-talk has been institutionalised as a major vocabulary of political discourse. (Fraser, 1989: 291)

For the purposes of critical evaluation, we highlight three features of Fraser's analysis and consider the place of evaluation within them:

- a focus on discourses of needs rather than needs objectively or subjectively defined;
- attention to competing discourses of needs and oppositional struggles intended to place needs in the social sphere and have them regarded as legitimate;
- consideration of ways in which to make judgements about whether some interpretations of need are better than others.

Fraser shifts enquiry from a focus on need, and the effectiveness of practice in meeting this need, to a focus on discourses of need. She moves then from both a positivist approach which determines need objectively and an interpretivist approach which relies on subjective expressions of need. Her postmodernist approach is to look at the ways in which need is interpreted through a myriad of processes and to recognise the 'politics of need interpretation' (Fraser, 1989: 292). The interpretation of need is thus recognised as problematic and political.

The analysis reveals 'needs-talk' as politically contested. It matters and makes a difference as to who interprets need, from what perspectives and vested interests. Needs discourses are multivalent and contested: there are competing ways of talking about people's needs. However, 'some ways of talking about needs are institutionalised' (Fraser, 1989: 296) and thus authoritative definitions of people's needs become established. Other ways of talking about needs become excluded, marginalised or co-opted within prevailing discourses. Competing discourses are played out in a society of inequality, a society stratified by dimensions of class, race, sexuality, age, disability and gender. Thus, discourses of need which serve to maintain existing power relations and the dominance of some over others become socially authorised and come to be regarded as adequate and fair.

To engage in the politics of 'needs-talk', to participate in the playing out of competing discourses, requires having the resources to do so, what Fraser terms as 'the socio-cultural means of interpretation and communication' (Fraser, 1989: 294). These resources are available to some and not others. They comprise, for example: officially recognised idioms; vocabularies such as therapeutic, materialistic, feminist, socialist; narrative conventions; modes of subjectification which construct people in such ways (professional, citizen, deviant, victim, user, etc.) as to provide them with more or less legitimacy and the capacity to have credible views; recognised arenas for resolving competing needs claims such as scientific expertise, local democratic systems, market place consumerism.

With these resources competing needs-claims are presented and alternative interpretations of need are continually articulated intended 'to challenge, displace, and/or modify dominant ones' (Fraser, 1989: 296). Thus, needs discourses are not a coherent monolithic web. Rather, in a stratified rather than a pluralist society, they constitute 'a heterogeneous, polyglot field of diverse possibilities and alternatives' (Fraser, 1989: 295).

Evaluation is a means of interpretation and communication more available for some than others. Through evaluation, needs are talked about in particular ways. Evaluation provides another vocabulary with which to talk about needs.

More than that, credibility and legitimacy may be attached to 'needs-talk' if it is framed in the language of evaluation, research and scientific analysis.

Second, Fraser situates these competing discourses with social-structural features. By 'political' Fraser not only refers to the officially recognised political sphere. Rather, she argues that the interpretation of need may be contested in any sphere: political, economic, domestic. In fact, the very process of defining the political sphere as distinct is a way of assigning an apolitical status to other spheres, the economic and domestic. This has the effect of depoliticising need in these spheres. So, for example, the closure of a factory becomes, in the economic sphere, the rational decision of economists; the rape of women in the home becomes, in the domestic sphere, a private arrangement within a marital relationship. Child care may be defined in terms of domestic need, the needs for children to be cared for full-time by their mothers; in terms of economic need, the needs of the labour market for women who are mothers; politically, the need for women to have their own incomes and engage in life as women not only as mothers. The playing out of competing discourses then becomes a process of shifting interpretations of need – as Fraser calls them, 'leaky, runaway discourses' – from their place in domestic and economic spheres to the social, the place where leaky, runaway needs become thwarted, co-opted or translated into claims for government provision:

> the social is the switchpoint for the meeting of heterogeneous contestants associated with a wide range of different discourse publics. (Fraser, 1989: 301)

The social sphere is where the policy agenda is fought, lost and won, through alliances of competing claims about needs. When needs are successfully contested politically and translated into claims for government provision, they may be described as social needs. These changing boundaries of needs discourses may be driven from below through oppositional needs-talk engaged in by groups such as pressure groups (e.g. Child Poverty Action Group, Children's Legal Centre), new social movements (e.g. Outrage!, Disability Action North East, women's groups, Black groups, grey power groups), voluntary organisations and community groups, interest groups (e.g. carers' groups). They may be driven from above through the needs-talk of politicians, experts and professionals.

Oppositional needs discourses are those when, for example:

- disabled people contest the need interpretations that maintain them in economically disadvantaged positions;
- women speak publicly about hitherto depoliticised needs arising in the private sphere claiming that these should be regarded as legitimate political issues;
- the boundaries between the political, economic and domestic spheres are contested as feminists have demonstrated the relationship between woman in the home as mother, nurturer and carer, and woman in low-paid, low status, untrained work as carer;
- alternative need interpretations are offered as grey power groups argue for access to leisure and education resources for older people;
- new discourse publics are created through which new interpretations of need are presented as children's rights groups have articulated needs about young people in residential care;
- new means of interpretation and communication are developed to articulate needs as feminists have articulated, and thus made visible, sexual harassment.

Oppositional discourses are resisted, thwarted, co-opted and marginalised in a range of ways to prevent effective challenges to the status quo. Fraser turns our attention to 'reprivatization discourses' (Fraser, 1989: 304) involving the privatising of issues that threaten to spill over into public discourse. Thus, for example, needs for residential or domiciliary care in Britain have been translated away from the social security system to those of the mixed economy of welfare and families; similarly, many child welfare needs have been renegotiated away from welfare monopolies towards courts and families. There are continual attempts to avert political demands for change in a society of increasing inequality by privatising public issues into the personal problems of, say, young single mothers, young 'yobs', people who are homeless, 'new age' travellers.

Evaluation may provide a mechanism through which needs are shifted from one sphere to another or reprivatised by their location in technical, rather than political, spheres. A critical evaluation, though, provides the possibility for alternative discourses of need to be presented, for previously private issues to be presented on the public agenda. A critical evaluation would be alert to the possibilities for strengthening oppositional discourses. In the next chapter, applying the work of Fox (1993), we consider ways in which this may be done.

Thirdly, Fraser is crystal clear about the requirement to choose between competing needs claims and also about the fact that some interpretations of need are 'better' than others:

> To say that needs are culturally constructed and discursively interpreted is not to say that any need interpretation is as good as any other. (Fraser 1989: 311–12)

Fraser proposes both procedural and conseqentialist factors to consider in judging between competing interpretations of need. Procedural factors are those to do with the processes through which needs come to be articulated and the extent to which these are inclusive or exclusive:

> the best need interpretations are those reached by means of communicative processes that most clearly approximate ideals of democracy, equality and fairness. (Fraser, 1989: 312)

Consequentialist considerations mean taking account of the outcomes of rival interpretations, whether these conform to patterns of domination and subordination and whether they move policy, provision and practice in the direction of equality. The best needs interpretations are those that do not disadvantage some groups at the expense of others, thereby balancing principles of democracy and equality.

These criteria of democracy and equality provide a way in which an evaluation that is critical may judge between competing claims. Judgements about whether the practice is 'good', 'good enough', 'poor' or 'corrupt' and choices made between competing interpretations may be made, bearing in mind the extent to which these have been articulated through democratic processes and whether the consequences of taking them on board will be in the direction of equality.

In respect of evaluating policies and practices under the 1989 Children Act, Hardiker *et al.* remark:

> The language of 'needs' (institutional model of welfare) sits oddly in our new residualist era, and it remains to be seen how it will be operationalised. . . . Taken together, this restricted definition of support for families and children in need constitutes the new ideology of residualism and this will continue to provide a challenge for good practices in child care. (Hardiker, Exton and Barker, 1991c: 356–7].

The following case example illustrates ways in which attention to discourses of need can provide a valuable framework for designing a critical evaluation.

Case example

Competing discourses about 'children in need' were contested politically as the Children Bill progressed through parliamentary and legislative processes. Some thought that the claims made for children's needs in the Children Bill were pitched too much in residualist terms, denoting pathology. Indeed, the use of the term 'children in need' can be understood as a means of 'reprivatizing' needs into residualising family support services (Masson, 1990).

The story of this political struggle has yet to be told, but needs were certainly politically contested through discourses constructed by different interest groups. Pressure group activity attempted to influence the shape of the needs discourse, to articulate alternative discourses of need, by developing an outline of values, strategic objectives, and implementation procedures, underpinning a more 'welfarist' approach to needs (In Need Implementation Group, 1991). Indeed, the work of this group inspired a high-ranking response from the Department of Health to the effect that 'in need' was not to be confined to children on the child protection register, even though thcse children were obviously also 'in need'. 'Social problem-solving' was also very much in evidence within discourses (Department of Health, 1989b; plus numerous volumes of Regulations & Guidance and Training Manuals, e.g. Shaw *et al.*, 1991). Similarly, competing discourses were also played out in local authority politics. Labour-controlled councils, in contrast to Conservative ones, engaged in needs-talk along social group and community-based lines (Gardner, 1992; Streather, 1989). Thus, presenting alternative discourses about 'children in need' was a means of staking political claims and contesting social welfare priorities.

Needs-talk did not stop with the passing of the Children Bill. Social services departments are now operationalising the requirements of the legislation in contrasting ways (Aldgate and Tunstill, 1993; Tunstill, 1994); some are being proactive, others more reactive. Tunstill (1994) evaluates provision for 'children in need' in terms of why, what and how services are provided and who gets these services.

> It is of course impossible to entirely separate the four respective issues because in any field of social policy there is inevitably a close relationship between political and professional ideology, research activity, policy design and implementation, and the ultimate perceptions and behaviour of users/clients. Family Support is no exception. (Tunstill, 1994: 1)

This encapsulates the argument that needs discourses are contested politically and that the 1989 Children Act attempted to shift the boundaries of this discourse. The prime responsibility for the upbringing of children is firmly located with parents. The State has a duty to help them discharge those responsibilities in a spirit of voluntary partnership, using ordinary services wherever possible. The new emphasis on the mixed economy of welfare is reinforced in the description of social services departments as enabling authorities, working with, and facilitating the work of, others across the local authority and in the independent sector (Hardiker, 1992a; 1994b).

Nevertheless, the family support duty is owed to a restricted group of children – those 'in need'. This is clearly a mechanism for residualising service provision. The political claims are pitched thus:

> local authorities are not expected to meet every individual need, but they are asked to identify the extent of need and then make decisions on the priorities for service provision in their area in the context of that information and their statutory duties. (Department of Health, 1991a: 7)

Research evidence indicates, not surprisingly, that local authorities are operationalising the requirements in different ways (Department of Health, 1993; 1994; Aldgate and Tunstill, 1993; Tunstill, 1994). A wide range of services is being offered. More priority is being given to family centres, domiciliary care, sponsored childminding, child protection services and various types of accommodation than to befriending and laundry services or out-of-school and holiday activities. However, developments in accessing and facilitating provisions in the mixed economy of welfare have been slow (Ozolins and Tunstill, 1994). An apparent hierarchy of access to services is emerging, child protection being given higher priority than, say, homelessness or early level 'needs'. Children seen to be at risk of harm or neglect are given priority over households disconnected by public utilities.

Family support services for children in need will continue to be the subject of political contests and claims, through competing needs-talk. At many levels attempts are being made to influence service provision in light of evaluations concerning inadequate service delivery. Political stakeholders continue to construct discourses by delineating the outlines of residualised services and the mixed economy of welfare. Alternative discourses exert pressure to translate 'need' into universal social provisions, rights and interests (In Need Implementation Group, 1991). These contests are complex and ever-changing. Vested interests and stakeholders should continue to be analysed in the social policy contexts of needs discourses. Attempts to change are well worth pursuing.

Hardiker and Barker (1994a) have evaluated child protection policies and practices under the new legislation. They show that family support services for children 'in need' have been used positively to counter coercion and promote packages of care to prevent children's entry to care or to facilitate their reunification with parents. They judge the practices to be 'good' by locating them in the policy contexts of the new legislation and agency strategic objectives, together with social worker professional values, knowledge and skills. Other evaluators (The Social Services Inspectorate and an external assessor) were more critical of the practices, arguing that the thresholds of intervention were probably too high, i.e. that 'too many' children were allowed to 'bump along' in disadvantaged circumstances or that gatekeeping to the use of 'accommodation' was too restrictive. These contrasting evaluations and their underlying premises are being taken on board by local authority members, managers, and officers (i.e. some of the stakeholders) to consider changes in policies and practices. The power contests are not clear-cut or tightly coherent but represent shifting coalitions of interests as child welfare services develop in the mixed economy of welfare in the 1990s.

Judgements about 'good' and 'poor' practices have to be placed in their social policy contexts. This is a way of locating powerful vested interests and their coalitions and divergences. Social work practices must be evaluated in relation to the welfare objectives which underpin them.

> For example, if a worker practises within an institutional model of welfare which identifies (welfare state) needs, yet the agency prioritises a case in relation to residualism and minimum intervention, the criteria of effectiveness may conflict. The level of prevention also indicates criteria for evaluation; for example, family therapy may be too intrusive an approach at the stage of primary prevention and an insufficient package of service for some high risk/high need families on the threshold of breakdown (tertiary prevention). (Hardiker, Exton and Barker, 1991b: 145).

Four themes for critical evaluation have been illustrated:

- discourses are contested politically;
- contrasting discourses are used as legislation is implemented differently by different local authorities;
- different discourses provide distinctive criteria for making judgements about 'good' and 'poor' practices and these in turn become part of political and social change processes;
- criteria for evaluation must locate discourses in social policy contexts and take on board that these shape and construct the objectives of practices.

The next case example focuses on needs-led assessments within the 1990 NHS and Community Care Act. The language of needs is very evident in community care legislation and may be evaluated through discourse analysis.

Here, the new political economy is brought into even sharper relief than in the 1989 Children Act. As Walker (1989) argues, community care illustrates the breakdown in the precarious social democratic consensus associated with the neoliberal philosophy of the Thatcher Government, namely:

- antagonism towards public spending on the Welfare State;
- increased emphasis on self-help and family support;
- extension of the market and commodification of social relations.

The spillout in community care was evident in: the shift in local authority responsibilities from providing to enabling; decanting and dehospitalisation; residualising social services in relation to universalist-based provisions. As Walker (1989) observes, though, social services had never been anything but residual in respect of the totality of social care.

Hallett (1991) argues that the political process was foreshortened in community care compared with that evident in children's legislation. She cites the brevity of The Griffiths Report (1988) and the relative lack of research evidence in comparison with the Children Act. There was, however, quite a strong research base underpinning the community care White Paper and its implementation (see, for example: National Institute for Social Work, 1988, Sinclair *et al.*, 1990; Personal Social Services Research Unit publications; Robbins, 1993). Whatever the scale and pace of the influences, the political stakeholders and claims need to be explored. The illustrative case example below is confined to 'needs-led assessments', a central plank of the reforms.

Community care had been a political topic for over thirty years in Britain, so what specific coalitions of interests underpinned this legislative change? The following have been cited: the changing nature of the older population;

housing problems and poverty; disability pressure groups; the needs of carers; the political agenda. The spiralling social security budget for residential care and the 'perverse incentive' to choose this option rather than a domiciliary one crystallised all these concerns.

Needs-led assessments represent a discourse which identifies the boundaries of permitted and required practices in community care. Such assessments are not in any way claims to infinite needs-satisfactions. Some of the key issues in the White Paper 'Caring for People' (Department of Health, 1989a) and Practice Guidance from a social services department (Anyshire Social Services Department, 1993) are outlined in this case example.

Case example

In the White Paper, several issues in the political economy of community care are identified.

- First, given the social security arrangements there was a perverse incentive to choose residential and nursing home care rather than services for people at home. Services should intervene no more than is necessary to foster independence and should be targeted on those with the greatest needs.
- Second, proper needs-led assessments and good case management are to be made the cornerstone of high-quality care, within the context of developing a flourishing independent sector and securing value for money.
- Third, criteria for eligibility for assessment and the processes involved should be clearly publicised. These will be made in the context of stated objectives and priorities determined by the local authority.
- Fourth, local authorities will need to retain capacity to be direct providers of services for people with high levels of dependency or particularly challenging patterns of behaviour.
- Finally, local authorities will continue to meet the full cost of maintaining people in authorities' own homes,

> including costs of accommodation and food; all authorities will, therefore, need to review the extent to which they need to maintain homes of their own. Individuals in private and voluntary residential and nursing homes will be able to claim Income Support and Housing Benefit. Therefore, for example, in residential care the 'carrot' is that placing people in private homes should become cheaper; the 'stick' is that councils will bear the whole costs of placement in their own homes. This is one of the means by which the Government hopes that councils will come to reduce their own provision (Community Care, 1989).

Thus, the new discourse is pitched in terms of the mixed economy of welfare, needs-led assessments and case management, eligibility criteria and targeting, the residualisation of services provided directly by the local authority and the 'unlevel playing field'. People with their own private resources to purchase services will not have their needs assessed, which is not to say they have no needs.

In the Practice Guidance of one social services department this discourse is illustrated very specifically (Anyshire Social Services Department, 1993).

- First, whereas service-led assessments were often influenced by the route by which a referral was received, needs-led assessments are intended to be flexible and sensitive to users and carers needs, though these assessments will still be finite exercises. There will be constraints on choice given budgetary limits and the outcome of the assessment.
- Second, there are to be clearly identified criteria for eligibility and priority groups. Services will be targeted on those in greatest need.
- Third, the social security regulations, explained above, are elaborated in terms of limits to choice of accommodation: i.e. it must be suitable to a user's assessed need; it must not cost the local authority more than it would normally pay for accommodation for someone with the same needs; it must be available and the

provider must be willing to contract to the authority's usual terms and conditions.
- Finally, unmet need should be recorded and proformas are provided for needs-led assessments and care packages.

The boundaries of this needs discourse include: health and social care; social security and social services departments; the state, the family and the mixed economy of welfare. Needs-assessments operate as levers to redirect services away from residential to domiciliary care and from social services to independent sector provision. The rhetoric is shot through at every point by political economy: rationing, prioritising and targeting in order to secure 'value-for-money' and effective performance. Thus, it is through the language of needs-led assessments that these radical changes are to be made.

These parts of the legislation were not implemented until 1 April 1993. Research evidence on the new arrangements is beginning to filter through, though some of the best evidence on implementation is to be found in the national and professional press. Again, as with the 1989 Children Act, local authorities are operationalising the requirements in different ways. These are being closely monitored by the Social Services Inspectorate (Department of Health, 1992). Some are being proactive, others reactive, but all are influenced by the new limits on service developments required by political economy. Specific interests challenged include:

- the needs of some long-stay patients who used to receive 'free' NHS care and are now required to pay for their social care;
- disabled people have important rights outlined in legislation although these are curtailed by some needs-led assessments acting as a thin disguise for resource-led assessment rationed by criteria (Morris, 1993);
- the slow pace of change regarding support for carers (Warner, 1994);
- the threat to the profits of some markets in the independent sector;

- the needs of discharged mentally ill people living unsupervised in the community.

It will take some time to evaluate which of these trends are long-term or short-term, which groups are powerful enough to stake their claims and which are not, and what influences are brought to bear in processes of change.

Preliminary findings from one evaluation indicate that the new arrangements have transformed the priority given to adult services (elderly, disabled, learning disability and mental health). These have been elevated by the new legislation. The private domiciliary market is developing slowly. Needs-led assessments are beginning to free participants from some of the shackles of service-led provisions. The respective choices and expectations of users/carers and purchasers/providers are being addressed in varying ways (Hardiker and Barker, 1994b). Change in policy and practice is being facilitated by developments in community care planning, carer support groups, complaints procedures and interprofessional collaboration. These parallel some developmental work reported in the literature (Barnes and Wistow, 1994; Whittaker, 1994).

Clearly, judgements about 'good' and 'poor' practices have to be made in relation to the social policy contexts of welfare services. Political economy has changed the goal posts of service objectives and provisions and these delineate the contours for evaluation. However, this is not to say that there are not some 'fundamental' values by which policies and practices may be judged. We return to this issue in Chapter 8.

We have argued that needs-discourses are one means of staking political claims. They are contested politically through discourses constructed by those who wield and forge different types and degrees of power. The boundaries of these needs discourses shift accordingly both historically and socio-politically (Fraser, 1989; Layder, 1993). These issues are brought into sharp relief in social services departments as they struggle to survive in their turbulent environments. These welfare contexts have been turned around in the past decade as local authority members and personnel have had to address the new political economy, an ageing population, equality claims made by people and interest groups, and new legislation. Discourses are not 'just talk' but constitute powerful social realities such as shifting coalitions of interests, organisational changes and new developments in welfare practices. As the case examples show, the contours of these structural imperatives are illustrated by shifting boundaries between parents, families, the state and the law in child care; also, social security, social services, families and markets in community care.

The following case example bears testimony to these imperatives. It is drawn from an evaluation of an organisational change (known departmentally as Impetus for Change, or IFC) (Hardiker, 1992b).

Case example

With radical organisational change, members of the Social Services Committee promised to evaluate developments after one year, partly to monitor them and partly to engage politically with the officers involved. As they put it: to gauge their reactions, to applaud their achievements and to share solutions. A preliminary evaluation and literature review on performance measurement were undertaken. These were intended to provide a baseline for a fuller evaluation which would combine performance measures with a user survey and a further excavation of officers' reactions. The officers' responses to change at every level of the organisation were focused upon. The design of the evaluation was such that it would develop as a team-building exercise. The principles of the reorganisation were used as a focus for the evaluation. These were:

- user-led services;
- needs-sensitive services;

- generic access and one-stop, courteous, quick response;
- specialisms – building skills, knowledge and experience in relation to needs and activities;
- interprofessional and inter-agency collaboration.

The social services teams responded to a schedule, indicating progress and lack of progress for each of these principles. The data were analysed qualitatively to capture what the teams were conveying, using codes, themes and analytic induction (Burgess, 1984). There was agreement within teams about progress in areas of complaints, needs-based services, recruitment, Black resources teams, access response rates and reception, growth of specialisms and planning and collaboration in relation to community care and children's services. Areas where further progress was needed included: performance measurement, resource provision, implementation chains, training, evaluation, strategic planning and structural impediments (e.g. gatekeeping at access). Comments render these summaries rather more imaginatively:

'There is a dilemma between the "I can do culture" and the need to prioritise.'

'The Department needs a Race and/or Equal Opportunity Strategy to give direction and prioritise work.'

'We do not want to become an information, reception, screening service.'

'There is evidence that a more specialist approach is improving services and ensuring that greater priority is afforded to adult services than was previously the case.'

'We've lost some of the momentum on some issues that were predominant prior to IFC: equality targets, training, corporate working amongst specialist teams.'

'There is some difficulty sorting changes from IFC from the new legislation which drives us in this direction, although the former was meant to facilitate the latter. It is now a real question whether it does so sufficiently.'

'With any major organisational change, the main focus during the first six months or so is inevitably the management of change. To maintain services at the previous level is a reasonable achievement, given the energy which has to be invested in reorganising and in continual evaluation.'

The evaluation indicated that there were many good features represented by this organisational change (IFC). These included:

- the political processes which facilitated the changes, e.g. members' support plus negotiations with professional and union interests plus user groups;
- the ways IFC managed to place the agency in readiness for the massive changes required by new legislative imperatives, even anticipating the need to develop purchaser/provider arrangements and requirements for devolved budgeting;
- an acknowledgement that there are inevitably winners and losers in such upheavals and that organisational change is inherently a painful process;
- the authoritative intentions of members and senior managers began to impact on practice and practitioners also continued to influence policy development.

The evaluation concluded with some dissemination exercises, and discussions in relation to recommendations for change took place between the evaluator and the management team. An evaluation report was submitted to members and with change recommendations. Progress continued to be made in many of the areas identified. For example: one senior manager responsible for equal opportunities was seconded to the Chief Executive's Department to steer further developments; work continued to be undertaken in relation to performance measurement and user/carer involvement.

In this chapter we have attempted to develop our approach to evaluation by focusing upon needs-discourses and by adopting a methodology akin to Layder's research strategy (Layder, 1993). We have provided illustrative case examples on ways to analyse needs-discourses by 'reading' the texts of legislation, departmental guidance, the research literature and by using our own 'insider' knowledge. We derive the latter from our membership of several networks: academic (research and teaching); professional; pressure groups; policy communities, etc. We have explored the politically contested nature of needs-discourses, the shifting boundaries by and in which they are located, and the criteria for making claims about better or worse needs discourses. This has been an exercise in theoretical and empirical analysis, weaving threads between the different layers of social life that constitute the social welfare scenes examined.

Our approach is shaped by our own biographical situations. Our educational and professional lives have spanned the welfare state era and this creates a litmus test for everything we read, analyse and evaluate. Our lenses and yours focus upon these issues from different perspectives with different texts. At many points we have compared contemporary political economy with the welfare state society which we knew and applauded while at the same time being critical. The needs-discourses and theoretical analyses of us all will be biased in different ways, but biased they will be. We say this to remind ourselves and our readers that there is no one truth. Our readings and understandings are shaped by our biographies: biographies constructed through discourses, even though we have endeavoured to ply our craft using all the intellectual values, knowledge and skills we can muster (Mills, 1959). Being explicit about these things does not eradicate the biases in our work; it merely reminds us to reflect upon them.

7

Generating Evidence About Practice

Having developed possible frameworks for evaluation designs, in this chapter we focus upon developing evaluation methods. In particular, we intend to explore ways to undertake evaluations that are critical and informed with understandings of power and powerlessness. We consider ways in which to generate evidence about the practice being evaluated. We then proceed, in the following chapter, to look at ways in which such evidence may be analysed and used to inform the making of judgements about whether the practice is 'good', 'good enough', 'poor' or 'corrupt'.

Ongoing, serial evaluation

In the conclusions to Chapter 5, we acknowledged the need for ongoing, continuing evaluative processes producing, and supplemented with, one-off evaluations. We argued that a critical approach to evaluation would be best pursued through the organisation or project becoming evaluative and engaging in a series of evaluations. It is this approach to evaluation that informs this chapter.

In distinguishing between ongoing evaluation and serial evaluation we are mindful of two things. First, a difficulty is raised in ongoing evaluation by those involved in the processes getting used to them, treating them as procedural devices. After a time, such processes may cease to produce evidence of practice and instead become expressions of what workers and managers have learnt to say about practice. House, in Alkin (1990), raises similar questions:

> The question I have, and it is a question, is when the information system, the evaluation system, becomes highly routinised, does it lose a lot of its force, so that you're not asking important questions anymore? The evaluation forms may themselves produce information that covers up questions the respondents have. . . . you almost need to come in and change it every so often, just to throw people off balance. (House, in Alkin, 1990: 146)

We are faced with difficulties. On the one hand, we argue that evaluation should engage with practice in ongoing and informative ways, becoming part of the responsibilities of practitioners. On the other, we are aware of the tendency for in-house processes to become routinised and bureaucratised to such an extent that they act, not to reveal difficulties, conflicts or even failures in practice, but to cover up these things. Our task, then, in seeking to develop ways to generate evidence of practice, is to address this difficulty: paraphrasing House, our task is 'to throw routine off balance'.

One way is to develop ongoing evaluative processes linked to serial evaluation. As Patton remarked in the same debate with House and others:

> 'Ongoing evaluation' still needs some discrete stopping places to figure out what has happened over time. (Patton, in Alkin, 1990: 150)

Another reason for serial evaluation is that not everything can be evaluated at once. Although it is vital that practice is evaluated in context and the 'totality' of practice taken into account, at the same time it is not feasible to evaluate everything. Decisions need to be made as to what is to be evaluated, what aspect of the organisation's work is to be scrutinised. In one-off evaluations this poses a difficulty. In serial evaluation, the issue is what to evaluate this time round. Thus, a distinction may be made between ongoing evaluative processes and a series of evaluations focusing on specific aspects.

Practice and the practitioner

Through our text, we have moved from positivist notions of practice as a discrete activity that may be objectively studied to a critical, postmodernist understanding of practice. This recognises ways in which practice is constructed and given meaning by actors through processes. Furthermore practice does not stay still. It is constantly negotiated, reformulated, redefined and prioritised by these actors and processes. Meaning can only be attributed to practice, or, in other words, we can only understand what is going on, if we tease out the discourses of practice. In this, we must inform our investigations and the resulting information with understandings of power. This has been well illustrated in the previous chapter with reference to discourses of need (Fraser, 1989).

Practice is not a discrete entity that may be studied separately from the competing discourses through which it is formed. Of the actors involved in practice, we need to study their practices, their words, their meanings, their intentions, purposes, what they expect to happen through practising in a particular way, why they have chosen to practise in that way rather than another. This is about teasing out the theories that inform practice: these may be implicit and contradictory. The process of generating evidence about practice is one of making these theories explicit. The evaluative process becomes one of enabling, through dialogue, those involved in the practice to reflect critically in an informed way on what is happening. It becomes a process of deconstructing discourses so that what appears to be the 'authoritative' case is not adopted uncritically without question. It is about 'throwing routine off balance' (House, 1990).

Guba and Lincoln (1989) suggest that evaluations should focus upon areas of actual or potential conflict and disagreement rather than only upon those areas where there is agreement. They propose examining stakeholders' claims, concerns and issues. Claims are assertions that the practice is 'good' or 'good enough'. Concerns are assertions made by stakeholders that the practice is 'poor' or even 'corrupt'. Issues are defined as 'any state of affairs about which reasonable persons may disagree' (Guba and Lincoln, 1989: 40). They provide as examples the introduction of AIDS education in first schools and the place of religious instruction in schools In other words, issues are aspects of practice already recognised as political. Fraser (1989), however, has warned us of only focusing upon those issues already accepted within the political sphere. Adopting a critical approach which examines the formation of powerful discourses and discursive fields, we are as concerned to scrutinise supposedly agreed practices as those where there is recognised and articulated disagreement.

Practice of course should not be de-contextualised. The actors involved in it and the processes in which they are engaged are required and informed by, named and legitimated through social, economic, political and legal processes. The continuing negotiations of those involved in practice take place within these contexts and indeed contribute to their construction. Policy and legal contexts are not set from on high in such a way as to pull the strings of actors in practice as though merely puppets. Context and practice are both continually constructed through social and political processes.

Case example

Following the implementation of the 1989 Children Act, an evaluation was undertaken in a social services department to judge the appropriateness of ways in which social workers identified thresholds in significant harm. In generating evidence of the practice data were collected to build up the evolving but coherent picture of the legitimating context for their practice. The evaluators started by scrutinising the 1989 Children Act and the social services department child care strategy. They sought out the conceptual building blocks of the 1989 Children Act and the principles underlying the social services strategy. The picture that emerged illustrated the non-interventionist principle, the shift towards legalism, changes in the balance of power between families and the state, concern for the welfare of the child and for acting in partnership with parents. Conflicts emerged in that the perspectives of the social services department and the evaluators differed from the views of the social services inspector and another 'welfarist' evaluator. Judgements differed about the appropriateness of levels of intervention in relation to 'degrees' of significant harm. Through the evaluation, though, the practice of the social workers demonstrated accountability to professional values and revealed knowledge and skills in the context of the new legislation and the policy directives of the organisation. (Hardiker and Barker, 1994a)

This example illustrates the nature of practice, the place of different perspectives of stakeholders and the ways in which evaluation must take account of context. Practice is continually negotiated by the actors involved in it in contexts which themselves are constructed through social and political processes. We place particular emphasis on the need for the practitioner to take responsibility for evaluating for 'good' practice. This is not to deny what we have been saying about stakeholders. All stakeholders have a right to be involved in evaluating practice, but, in our view, practitioners also have a responsibility to do so.

At the same time, we must not treat practitioners as benign. Practitioners are powerful. It is as much through their language, their codes of expertise, their processes and interactions that discourses of practice are formed as through policies, procedures and mechanisms set from on high. Practitioners too may involve themselves in and/or collude with 'corrupt' practice.

Understanding methods

Before proceeding with an exploration of methods, two points must be clarified. First, it is important to constantly bear in mind that methods should not be taken out of context. Methods have to be theorised and politicised. Otherwise, they will become techniques ready to be captured by prevailing powerful processes while at the same time providing no possibility for revealing the values with which they are laden. We demonstrated this in Chapter 4 in our scrutiny of supposedly technical methods of measuring performance.

Second, methods should not be equated with particular approaches. Often, for example, qualitative methods such as participant observation and biographical methods are equated with interpretivism. While it is the case that these methods may be appropriate for exploring people's subjective experiences, they may also be implemented within positivist and critical social science paradigms.

Asking users, for example, does not necessarily imply engaging in interpretative qualitative interviewing. Nor are user consultation exercises necessarily best conducted in participative ways. It may sometimes be more revealing to conduct a more independent survey of a sample of users. We must not forget that it can sometimes be easier, and less controlling, to tell it all to a third party, perhaps an interviewer who seemingly has nothing to do with the organisation and/or with the particular worker. The meaning of method has to be appraised and clarified to ensure that the method fits the purpose of the evaluation exercise (Brannen, 1992).

We illustrate our approach to methods by looking at alternative ways of seeking the views of users. Also, through this exercise we portray ways in which discourses, and languages within them, serve both to maintain and strengthen power and inequality and provide ways in which power and powerful processes are resisted and challenged.

We wish to show how important it is to analyse critically why users are asked about their experiences of the service or project. Advocating the need to listen to users may appear to be democratic and potentially radical. However, in engaging in user studies of satisfaction, organisations may be doing more to confirm existing power relations than to change them. And this may be as much the case for the large statutory organisation as for the small voluntary and community-based project (Sainsbury, 1987).

Asking users

User studies have emphasised the importance of listening to users of services, learning from their experiences, providing them with opportunity to comment on services and contribute to their development. There have been interesting innovatory evaluations that have provided funding for users to conduct their own evaluations. For example, the Model Cities Administration in the United States provided resources for neighbourhood groups

> to study the program from their own perspective and thereby satisfy their own interests, information needs, and criteria of success. (Weiss, 1986b: 149)

However, the success of such schemes is often limited, with users prioritising social action, social change and provision of resources rather than evaluation *per se.*

More commonly, user studies mean professional practitioners, evaluators and researchers asking users about their experiences of the programme, project or practice. It cannot be denied that it is good practice to consult users and check out with them their experiences of the services. In these respects, the 1990 National Health Service and Community Care Act and the 1989 Children Act are important. Together with initiatives such as the Citizen's Charter the new legislation places emphasis on seeking the views of users and carers on the planning, delivery and management of services and on providing complaints procedures.

In its local authority guidance on Community Care inspection, the Department of Health suggests that users' experiences of services should be the major focus for evaluations for the following reasons:

- on ethical and effectiveness grounds assuming that users know better than providers what a service has been like, although at the same time recognising that both users and providers have particular and valid views about quality;
- regarding participation in service specification and evaluation as allowing for a measure of influence over quality and quantity and as facilitating processes of mutual learning between providers and users;
- acknowledging that users and providers in the independent sectors pay and should be satisfied of value for money. (Department of Health, 1991b)

Furthermore, the Department of Health recommends that users be supported to become meaningfully involved in the inspection of services, through:

- the development of processes of open communication;
- the provision of facilitators, enablers and advocates;

- providing opportunities for training in assertiveness, communication and groupwork skills;
- the implementation of meaningful complaints procedures;
- the provision of information about inspection;
- consulting with users on their involvement in inspection;
- including users in monitoring systems;
- encouraging users, say residents in elderly persons' homes, to participate in reciprocal visits/inspections. (Department of Health, 1991b)

These are interesting and potentially valuable suggestions which could well be applied to critical evaluations. We will return to some of them later in the chapter. But again, it is important to attach meanings to methods and not take them out of context and at face value.

Coote (1994) provides a valuable analysis showing ways in which alternative discourses of performance and quality may all contribute to a discursive field which serves to co-opt users into prevailing values, thus thwarting any challenge to the status quo. The language of user-centred developments may not mean what it appears to at first sight. Alternative ways of seeking user views are deconstructed for ways in which they serve to ward off any challenge to the status quo and even serve to strengthen unaccountable managerial control.The 'scientific approach' measures users' expressions of satisfaction against pre-set standards through, for example, the mechanisms of the British Standards Institute. The evidence generated is in danger of being treated as though it were true, thus producing 'a regime of truth'. Such an approach may in fact assign power to experts of a different sort, experts in scientific management:

> they are laid down by experts, have an aura of scientific authenticity and are not generally negotiable. Moreover, this ap-

> proach is paternalistic. The experts are in control. They decide what is a 'given need'; they decide what is 'satisfaction'. (Coote, 1994: 188)

The 'managerial or excellence' approach focuses on what the customer wants, shifting power 'from professionals towards managers'. Through this approach:

> A wide range of decisions has passed into the domain of managerial discretion. Management as a 'science' is supposed to be value free and above politics but in fact it can be highly political, especially when it operates in the public sector. Unlike doctors and other professional groups, managers have no self-imposed code of ethics or practice. Nor are they directly accountable to the public. (Coote 1994: 190)

Thus, providing what the customer wants may have the effect of enhancing managerial control and decreasing public accountability. In the previous chapters, we have developed an understanding of the discourse of managerial evaluation, a collusion of rational-positivist scientific methods with new managerialism. Here, we see ways in which the discourse of customer satisfaction serves too to strengthen managerialism and control while on the face of it appearing to pass more say to users of social services.

Coote's critical alternative is to advocate a 'democratic' approach to quality. What distinguishes this from those already analysed is that it transfers power to those relatively powerless in the social welfare system. Instead of standards set through scientific management, Coote argues that the standard by which services should be judged is 'equity'.

We are straying here into the business of the next chapter: that is, how to make judgements about whether the practice is 'good', 'good enough' 'poor' or even 'corrupt'. The construction of the subject, the user, consumer, customer, through the language, policies and processes of discourses, is key to postmodernist thinking. So too is the possibility for resisting such constructions by promoting alternative discourses. The democratic model seeks to develop ways through which these constructions may be resisted through processes that accord rights to users.

We are still concerned to press the point that methods must be theorised and politicised in context. (And we have chosen to prioritise the contents of this 'methods' chapter thus because so often, in their effort to be accessible to practitioners, evaluation and research texts focus on methods exclusively to the extent that they become atheoretical and de-politicised.) Looking at different methods of seeking users' views strengthens the argument for the need to choose and develop methods to fit the purpose of the evaluation, in our case to employ evaluation methods that have a chance of helping to ensure 'good' practice.

Beresford and Croft (1993), distinguishing between 'democratic' and 'consumerist' approaches, argue for approaches to research and evaluation that provide opportunities for users to undertake their own research and participate in processes of research and evaluation. They suggest the following guidelines for participatory evaluation. It should:

- be linked to participatory initiatives from the start instead of being undertaken retrospectively as is often the case;
- be based on an action-research model where there is a continuing process of research informing change; and
- rest on a set of clear criteria, developed for assessing participatory initiatives, including exploration of participants' views, equal opportunities policies, participatory structures, conditions of involvement, rights and outcomes. (Beresford and Croft, 1993: 73–4)

We take this last point to mean that participatory initiatives and the action-research model should be constantly appraised to ensure continuing effectiveness in democratising evaluation processes. This is essential since discourses continually entwine language, processes, policies and strategies to produce 'regimes of truth'. And this includes discourses of participatory involvement just as much as any discourses. Thus, supposedly empowering processes must be constantly scrutinised, or deconstructed, through evaluation processes with a view to fostering alternative discourses that challenge inequality. So, for example, a voluntary project committed to user involvement and participatory strategies must be evaluated for the effect these have on power and powerlessness just as much as a social services department with explicit bureaucratic and managerial processes must be evaluated for the same purposes.

A further point needs to be made about the danger of equating participatory evaluation processes at local, community level with empowerment and critical practice. Sometimes a sample survey of users, non-participatory and seemingly within a positivist paradigm, may be more revealing of the experience of practice than any project-based participatory exercise. Judge and Solomon (1993), for example, report on patterns of consumer satisfaction of health services. They take their findings from large national surveys, such as the British Social Attitudes Surveys. These are undertaken regularly and include within them questions about people's attitudes to the health service. One important finding is that people consistently are more critical of services than they are of professionals. This mirrors what we have learnt from user studies in social work about the reluctance of clients to express any criticism of their social workers (Rees and Wallace, 1982).

The power of professionals and practitioners needs to be taken into account. It is not only managers and evaluators who are powerful. To be dependent on a social worker for a 'positive' assessment that will lead to the delivery of long-awaited home care services does not place a user in a strong position to be critical. To be dependent on a probation officer making a case in court that may lead to community service rather than imprisonment does not necessarily enhance the possibilities of the young person evaluating the service from their own experience (but see Willis, 1991). In being invited to express their views on the quality of service, clients, patients and users will talk as strategically as every other actor involved in practice. And such strategic talking, 'the politics of practice talk' (to paraphrase Fox, 1993), shows that users, as well as managers, practitioners and evaluators, can and do engage in powerful processes.

Furthermore, the closer to the experience of the service, the more likely it is that people express satisfaction with it. For example, recent experience of both in-patient and out-patient health services appears to enhance levels of satisfaction (Judge and Solomon, 1993). Perhaps the more you are able to distance yourself from the service, the more likely you are to be able to reflect on it and voice criticisms.

It is undoubtedly the case that people in trouble may, at first anyway, experience gratitude. Some people, because of their experiences of inequality and powerlessness, have lower expectations than others. So while a broad sample survey of users may be more effective in revealing patterns of user satisfaction than a small, project-based participative discussion, such a study needs to be complemented by more in-depth qualitative interviews. Judge and Solomon (1993), for example, reveal a picture of some complexity which confirms 'the importance of not considering opinions of health services in a political vacuum' (Judge and Solomon, 1993: 316). They find, for example:

- that, in all studies, older people express greater levels of satisfaction than do younger people;
- in some studies women express more satisfaction than men but in others there appears to be no gender difference;
- Black people express less satisfaction than do white, probably reflecting both experience and awareness of racial discrimination;

- lower socio-economic status 'seems to be associated with lower expectations and more acceptance of the status quo' (Judge and Solomon, 1993: 311);
- and people living in the North of England appear to be more satisfied with health services than do those in London and the South-East.

And yet what we know of inequality in health and health care must strengthen the view that

> it is essential to be both sensitive to the context in which people are approached, and cautious about the interpretations that can be drawn out from the information which people offer. There is potential for public agencies to become complacent if the replies of 'grateful' users are used in an uncritical way. It is important to examine the nature of people's assessments of public services, to acknowledge the political context in which attitudes are formed, and to attempt to investigate the variations in opinion within the population, in order to reach valid, sensible and useful conclusions. Exercises in consultation are important, but they need to be conducted with care and sensitivity if the views of consumers are to be taken seriously. (Judge and Solomon, 1993: 325)

Very interestingly, Judge and Solomon suggest that not only should views be theorised and politicised but also that the more 'educated' the person, the more confident they are to engage with the policy process in the evaluation of services. This provides us with the key to evaluation methods that may, both through the process and the findings of the evaluation, contribute to the development of 'good' practice. As well as using well tried and tested research methods, evaluation methods may also borrow from community education practices in order to address processes of power and powerlessness in social welfare.

Well-tried and tested research methods

There is a wealth of literature on methods of research as ways of generating evidence and increasingly many valuable texts written for practitioners intended to make the doing of research accessible. We have included an annotated bibliography of these in an appendix at the end of this book. This is adapted from the recent publication from ARVAC, *Making it Work: Researching in the Voluntary Sector* (Everitt and Gibson, 1994). There is therefore no need for us to take space here in elaborating further the vast array of methods of research for collecting data.

In this chapter we have used the term 'generating' rather than 'collecting' data as more appropriate for the inevitably interactive process involved in finding out what goes on in practice, from whose perspective, in what context. It is important to reflect on the myriad of ways in which data are generated through the routines of practice as well as using research methods to generate additional data. And, in deciding on the most effective ways of generating evidence of practice, it is vital to ensure that all with an interest in that practice have opportunity to have a say. In the previous section, we have argued for the importance of theorising views expressed in order to develop understandings of what people say, why, with what effects, with what experiences, in what contexts. In social welfare, we also have to consider carefully how to ensure that those who may not be verbally articulate or fluent in the English language are not excluded from the evaluation process. Thought must be given to the most effective ways of seeking information from people whose first language is not English, from children, from older people, from learning-disabled people (see Whittaker, 1994). And equally important is the need to think carefully about how to delve below official language and organisation 'speak'.

Case example

The evaluator embarked on a process to ascertain the views of young children living and going to primary school in that area. The projects were interested to know something more about the ways these children thought about their neighbourhood. The evaluator enlisted the help of the neighbourhood playworker and together they reached an agreement with the school to hold discussions with a group of seven-year-olds over a ten-week period. They got together a group of five boys and five girls and met with them separately and together. At first they tried to get the children to write about their neighbourhood, about the places they liked and those they disliked. However, this process, including the tasks of sharpening pencils and spelling out words, took longer than expected and the methods appeared to constrain the expression of views. After much thought, an alternative method was decided upon which, from both the experience of the project and the resulting exhibition of the children's views, was most effective. From the small evaluation budget, ten disposable cameras were purchased. Each child was given one for an afternoon and the evaluator and the playworker each took a group of five children to walk around the neighbourhood. The children took photographs of their favourite places – the park, the school playground – and those places they usually steered clear of – the bushes, the unlit areas, the main road. They photographed the places that they thought significant – the library, the old imposing Victorian buildings – and places where they or members of their families went as part of routine living in the area – the shops, the pubs, the different housing types. Then, once the photographs were processed, they together discussed the pictures, and the places, saying what they thought of them. Their words and pictures were put together in an exhibition that was taken from place to place, like the Civic Centre, the school, the community projects. Children's views were on the agenda. (Green, 1994)

This example shows the value of thinking imaginatively

about processes of generating data, and designing and implementing these processes to suit not only the purposes of the evaluation but also the people to be involved. Researchers talk about triangulation to mean the practice of generating data from a wide range of sources and using several methods of data collection. This is necessary in critical approaches which do not rely exclusively upon the perspectives of either policy-makers and managers or practitioners or users.

However, triangulation can be an invitation to generate an infinite variety and amount of data which in the end cannot be utilised for the evaluation. It is important to ensure that all relevant perspectives are included and the process of participating in an interactive data generation process can itself be valuable. But it is equally important to be careful about becoming submerged in data. Many potentially valuable studies reach an unfortunate premature end in this way! We do not advocate triangulation in order to capture the many (and moving) truths of practice. Triangulation for us is not a positivist notion that will pick up all the pieces and, through completing the jigsaw, create the final true picture of practice. What matters in a critical evaluation is that views are sought from those people who may never or seldom be heard and that practice is scrutinised to reveal patterns of domination and subordination. Social welfare in a democratic society has to be about working towards a society where each and every person is able to flourish as a human being, be concerned for the well-being of others and contribute to a society of equality and justice.

In designing an evaluation, issues of feasibility need to be taken into account. These will include designing the methods to fit the purpose of the evaluation, whether it is ongoing, serial or one-off. The resources available for the evaluation have to be carefully allocated, and they are always limited. The evaluation must be manageable. Permission will need to be sought from people expected to provide information. People's views and experiences belong to them and care needs to be taken in inviting people to participate. Thought needs to be given to accessing information and views. Some people of course may adopt the position of speaking for others in this respect. There are those who act as gatekeepers to data in the form of committee papers, diaries, files, case-notes, etc. There are also those who act as gatekeepers to people. Permission may need to be sought from teachers and/or parents to talk to schoolchildren, from social workers to talk to clients, from prison officers to talk to prisoners, from managers to talk to practitioners. Strategies may need to be employed to ensure that all who should have a say through the evaluation do so.

Dialogical methods

In developing a postmodern theory of health, Fox (1993) conceptualises practice as 'the politics of health-talk' implying an interest in discourse and its consequences for power, control and domination. He identifies the following themes:

- an interest in deconstructing discourses and discursive formations;
- an understanding of the ways in which subjectivity is constructed through discourse, knowledge and power with a recognition that power can be positive in resistance and contestation;
- a scepticism of common sense and the taken-for-granted;
- an interest in the relationship between desire and discourse;
- a focus upon intertextuality and reflexiveness in the production of personal texts. (Fox, 1993: 19)

These themes provide us with ways to think about developing evaluation methods that will contribute to the creation of alternative discourses and will 'throw routine off balance' (House, in Alkin 1990) to develop practice in the direction of the 'good'.

Through Coote's analysis of approaches to user satisfaction we have illustrated ways in which discourses may and must be deconstructed to reveal them as processes of power and domination. We have argued in the previous chapter, and illustrated in this one, that discourses affect the truth and have the effect of acting as 'regimes of truth'. Commonsense and taken-for-granted routines are discourses that need to be made explicit and scrutinised for the ways in which they make us think that particular ways of understanding personal troubles and social ills are true and therefore not contested. This is the task of evaluation, through both ongoing evaluative mechanisms and serial evaluations. But the task we have set for ourselves is that evaluation should not only deconstruct but also should contribute to people acting positively.

Fox's use of the notion of desire and his thinking about intertextuality suggest ways in which dialogical methods may be used to resist powerful discourses. Feelings of desire indicate that people are not totally passive, not totally subjected by powerful discourses. This is not to say that there is an essential subject outside of discourses but rather that within each of us is a desire to resist being totally territorialised. This desire relates to the capacity of people to act and to resist. It is about the subject, although constituted through language, processes, behaviours and practices, becoming empowered. It is about being able to think and act autonomously, and by so doing engage in the creation of alternative discourses. It is about 'thinking and practising otherwise' (Hardiker, 1994a). It indicates the subject as active. Of course, this does not mean necessarily acting in the direction of the good. The will to power must constantly be reflected upon, but we return to this issue in the next chapter where we focus upon making judgements about 'good' practice.

As Fox explains, 'this emphasis upon desire as the primary force opens up a politics of resistance' (Fox, 1993: 84). Fox gives examples of the ways in which people resist being contained within prescribed sick roles by engaging in behaviour and speaking words that refuse to conform to the routines established through health institutions, professionals and practices (see also Hardiker *et al.*, 1986). Evaluation methods, by asking the questions that never should be asked, by giving people permission to say what never should be said, can attend to desire rather than confirm 'the will to power' as in managerial evaluation. Evaluation becomes a process of puncturing established frameworks of meaning: of 'throwing routine off balance' (House, in Alkin 1990).

Evaluation becomes a dialogical process providing opportunities for all, practitioners and users alike, to reflect upon and understand the meaning of their experiences. This is with a view to deepening those understandings to take account of ways in which they have been shaped through discourses.

Fox (1993) develops the practice of intertextuality as a form of reflective activity. In some ways, this approach can be likened to the work of Freire (1972) in providing opportunities for people to create texts of their own lives in order to counter the texts that have been foisted upon them through systems of domination such as colonialism. The process is one of becoming reflective, countering the ways in which we are thought about, and come to think about ourselves, by producing alternative versions, different accounts, new possibilities. Rather than producing the truth, writing, creating the text, is a way of constructing an account which itself can be reflected upon and changed. It is not a process of producing a permanent, unchangeable alternative for this itself would merely serve to reproduce a 'regime of truth', even though a different one.

Writing a text is to produce something which is recreated by the reader, even by self, on re-reading:

> As an intertextual practice, writing has particular attractions. Writing provides a forum for positive agency: space to act in a world where it is more usual to be the subject of writing. Writing's relative permanence paradoxically makes it less permanent – able to be changed, rubbed out, refined or trashed. Writing enables reflection: it can be returned to, contextualised, reread. In addition, writing can be deconstructed. (Fox, 1993: 110)

Evaluation methods can provide opportunities for people involved in the project, in receipt of the service, to create the text of their experiences. This is quite a different approach to asking users what they want or asking about levels of satisfaction. It is a dialogical approach that combines processes of questioning with social and cultural practices in the pursuit of reflection, learning and autonomy (Whittaker, 1994).

Dialogical methods can be used to enable people to reflect on their experiences and develop understandings. Experiences, and reflections on them, may not necessarily be in the form of written texts. We can learn from feminist consciousness-raising groups and from practitioners in community education, for example. There are a myriad of ways in which people can make visible their experiences, to themselves as well as to each other. The evaluators talking with children soon realised what a tortuous process it can be to rely upon writing! The evaluation of the EC NOW funded Newcastle Women's Network employed a range of methods to ensure that the perspectives of women trainees on social and economic exclusion were acknowledged and that, through the evaluation, these women had the opportunity to learn about the place of education and training in addressing exclusion:

Case example

In one session during the women's training programme a video extract from a recent magazine-style programme on educational issues was presented for group discussion. The extract was of a case of a failing school in a black inner-city community in America. In a radical attempt to reverse the school's fortunes, a private company was awarded a contract to manage the school. The extract showed the new management's controversial approach to raising educational standards, starting with improving children's self-esteem using behaviourial learning techniques.

The extract was stopped at regular intervals to encourage discussion, and the following questions were posed to help the women trainees reflect on and analyse what they were seeing:

1. What is happening in this part of the extract?
2. How do I feel about what I am seeing?
3. What similarities can I see with my own experiences of schooling, either as a learner or as a parent?
4. What differences can I see with my own experiences of schooling, either as a learner or as a parent?
5. How worthwhile would these approaches be in tackling the problems in our schools?

The discussion enabled women to discuss the relationship of school to the community and to society in general. Particular issues such as the importance of self-esteem in learning, relevance in the curriculum and the nature of 'good' teaching were debated.

In another session, the women trainees were asked to construct word pictures around six themes: family, childhood, health, community, youth, work. These were identified from in-depth interviews with women on their educational and work histories. Working in small groups, the women proposed and debated statements relating to each theme. These statements were recorded on flip-chart paper around the centrally written theme.

When the individual groups had completed their word

> pictures, the flip-chart pages were displayed around the room. Women viewed the work of other groups and added on whatever additional comments they wished to have recorded. The word pictures were viewed as glimpses of how women saw some aspects of their experience at the time.
>
> In the final phase of this constructivist exercise, the women trainees worked with a community photographer to turn their word pictures into visual images for the evaluation report. (NOW Joint Evaluation and Development Project, 1995)

This was a process through which people learned about their lives and the practices in which they are involved. It is perhaps a different educational approach to that advocated by the Department of Health in its recommendations for training to be provided for users to enable them to participate in Community Care quality systems (Department of Health, 1991b). But the legislative framework, together with the Departmental guidance, does provide a mandate for involving users in such educative processes.

Finally, we turn to thinking about evaluation methods that could be encouraged in organisations in their quest to become evaluative.

Supervision as an evaluative process

We need to think about building processes into organisations to develop them as evaluative. Having regard for the place of the practitioner in evaluation it is important that we develop some way to tease out their evidence of practice. In social work, probation and other professional areas such as midwifery there has been a tradition of supervision, an opportunity for practitioners to reflect on their practice with the help of their supervisor who may or may not be their line manager. In our view, a critical approach to supervision can provide evidence of practice invaluable for ensuring that the organisation or project is evaluative.

Carter *et al.* (1992) develop reflective supervision approaches for educating students on practice placements. The 'dialogical' model focuses upon the practitioner's experiences. It places emphasis on the practitioner being or becoming autonomous and it takes account of the context in which practitioners act. It is an approach to supervision that falls within the critical social science paradigm that informs our proposed critical evaluation:

> Experience, feelings and perceptions are understood as 'socially constructed', that is as arising in specific and complex political, economic, social and interpersonal contexts. They are thus interrogated through the use of 'dialogue' between supervisor and supervisee, examining the taken-for-granted. (Carter *et al.*, 1992: 51)

The dialogical model draws upon Smyth's model designed to encourage reflective thinking (Smyth, 1991). This we think provides ways in which to interrogate practice, to make explicit evidence of practice as we have defined it. In other words, the approach assumes that to find out about what is going on in practice it is necessary to tease out the thoughts, values, intentions and aspirations of the actors involved. Smyth's model has four elements:

- describing: providing descriptive information about practice;
  telling the story of practice;
  telling of the confusions, ambiguities, contradictions, unknowns;
  borrowing from Guba and Lincoln (1989), making the 'claims', raising the 'concerns' and tabling the 'issues' of practice;
- informing: unpacking the descriptions for their meanings;

revealing theories that otherwise may have remained implicit;
revealing values;

- confronting: thinking about how and why the practice has developed in the ways that it has and not in other ways;
thinking about what this tells us about predominant values contained within the practice;
contemplating on where these values come from and how they relate to the social, economic, cultural and political contexts in which the practice takes place;
reflecting on who loses and who gains through the practices;
deliberating on what and who acts to limit and constrain the practice and skew it in particular directions and interests;
- reconstructing: working out how practice may be developed in different ways in the direction of the 'good';
how practice may be democratised;
in what ways those rendered relatively powerless in our society and through our practices may be empowered.

This dialogical supervision process may be seen as a process of intertextuality discussed in the previous section. Now in the next chapter we explore ways in which evaluation, employing well tried and tested research methods and dialogical processes, may be developed to enable judgements to be made about whether practice is 'good', 'good enough', poor' or 'corrupt'.

8

Making Judgements and Effecting Change

In the end evaluation involves making judgements about value and effecting change in the direction of the 'good'. It is these two central features that distinguish evaluation from research. In this chapter we look at ways in which the evidence of practice generated for the evaluation may be analysed and used to inform the making of judgements about whether the practice is 'good', 'good enough', 'poor' or 'corrupt'. We also reflect upon ways in which evaluation may be used to facilitate changes in practice and policies in the direction of the 'good'.

We are keen to distinguish evaluation from research. Many texts about evaluation treat it as research. Of course it is the case that research may be value-driven and concerned with bringing about change. Critical social research is informed and motivated through theories and experiences of power and powerlessness. Feminist research, for example, starting with knowing that there is gender inequality serving to render women relatively powerless, has as its purpose the development of understandings to bring about change in patriarchal relations. Kelly, Burton and Regan make this clear in writing about the work of the Child Abuse Studies Unit:

> Our desire to do, and goal in doing, research is to create useful knowledge, knowledge which can be used by ourselves and others to 'make a difference'. (Kelly, Burton and Regan, 1994: 28)

So, too, research undertaken within other social movements, such as by and with disabled people and older people, focuses upon generating evidence and understandings of inequality to bring about change. Oliver writes, for example:

> Disability research should not be seen as a set of technical, objective procedures carried out by experts but part of the struggle by disabled people to challenge the oppression they currently experience in their daily lives. (Oliver, 1992: 102)

Action-research and other forms of policy research also relate to policy and practice change. But while we place evaluation within these critical research paradigms, not all research is necessarily concerned with making judgements about the value and worth of practice. This is exactly what evaluation is. Furthermore, change for the better, change towards enhancing equality and challenging oppression, is integral to a critical approach to evaluation.

The need for judgement-making

It is not surprising that evaluation and research are so often conflated and that many evaluation texts within a positivist paradigm make no mention of the process of making judgements about value. After all, such evaluations assume that the data generated through rational-technical research processes produce valid and reliable findings which can be considered to be the probable 'truth' of that practice. There is no more to be said. There is no need for judgement-making about effectiveness. Effectiveness is proved, or not! Decisions about whether and to what extent the practice is achieving its intended objectives are made through processes of measurement and reasoning, through rational processes. This 'truth' is then presented to those who have commissioned the evaluation, usually people in powerful positions with regard to the making of policy and resource allocation decisions. These people will then be informed by the findings from the evaluation and make decisions to effect the necessary changes – so the rational story goes!

The model is neat and tidy, but there are several difficulties with it that make practitioners and others rightly sceptical. We have spelt these out throughout this text and so need only to summarise them here.

- First, 'truth' is not produced, but rather an interpretation of the practice is made. In the rational-technical approach, this interpretation is within the province of the evaluator, a province often shared with the commissioning agent to produce managerial evaluation.
- Second, objectives of practice are not fixed and given. To assume so is to accept and help maintain the status quo in a world divided unequally through dimensions of gender, race, age, disability, social class and sexuality.
- Third, the assumed rationality of decision-making informed by evaluation findings masks the complexity of the process and that the process is political involving the allocation of scarce resources to meet needs requiring definition and negotiation.
- Fourth, all these difficulties are underpinned by power being neglected to such an extent that a collusion results in managerial evaluation. This acts as a powerful form of organisational control. Not only does it bring about a surveillance of practice at a time of massive inequality, budget rationing and privatisation, but also it staves off any possible threat to the status quo and existing power relations which a critical scrutiny of practice may bring with it.

An interpretivist approach to evaluation does not provide the answer. When it comes to making judgements about the value of the practice, interpretivist evaluators are left with a problem. Their work results in the production of many truths of practice. Each actor or stakeholder may see the practice differently and value it in diverse ways. Smith and Cantley (1985), for example, in evaluating a psychogeriatric day hospital, sought the views of health board officials, specialist advisers, medical professionals, nurses and relatives of patients. They also examined hospital records and observed and recorded meetings of relatives and staff meetings. They claim that, in

> taking a sympathetic account of as many perspectives as possible, [their] pluralistic evaluation stands some chance of remaining 'independent' and neutral'. (Smith and Cantley, 1985: 81)

Smith and Cantley also claim that evaluation findings are much more likely to be taken on board when everyone involved has had a say. They do though acknowledge difficulties within their model, such as how to decide, and who should decide, whose views should be sought. Patients were an obvious omission in their study. But so also might some staff and relatives be excluded because of structural dimensions such as social class, gender, race, age, disability and sexual orientation rendering them marginal. A theory of power and exclusion is needed to guide the evaluator in the effort to ensure that some stakeholders are not systematically excluded.

Smith and Cantley also acknowledge that their approach may only be relevant when evaluating practice in contexts of consensus. It may not be adequate where there are observable conflicts of interest or, even more so, where conflicts of interest are not visible or articulated. A critical theory approach to evaluation would assume a conflict of interests and, in theorising power and powerlessness, would seek to ensure that some people are not excluded from the opportunity to express their views.

Evaluators informed by critical theory also depend on processes of reasoning to make value judgements. They also would argue that evaluation can produce the 'truth' of practice. But for them values and theories of power are built into the process from start to finish. These evaluators take account of ways in which subjective experiences and views are constructed in societies divided by gender, race, sexual orientation, age, disability and social class. However, their theorising about ideology and their dialogical methodologies of consciousness-raising present them with possibilities for the lifting of ideological influences to reveal true experiences and opinions. The reasoning process to reach the truth of the practice being evaluated becomes an educational as well as a research process providing people involved in the practice with opportunities for consciousness-raising to understand their true experiences of that practice.

Critical evaluators informed by postmodernist theories would understand the ways in which subjectivity is constructed. They would regard 'truth' as something which is strived for but yet never attained. These evaluators would understand the complexity and multiplicity of the many truths of practice. The role of the evaluator becomes one of deconstructing what comes to be known as the truth of practice, the powerful knowledge of discourses, while at the same time providing opportunities for alternative discourses to be articulated. Fraser (1989) uses the term 'needs-talk' to portray discourses of need. She shows very clearly that, while there is no one truth about need, 'needs-talk' serves to produce discourses which, unless deconstructed, may become regarded as truths acting in powerful ways to objectify others into need categories. Fox (1993) similarly uses the term 'the politics of health-talk or illness talk' in referring to the discourses of health practice.

In Chapter 6 we illustrated ways in which an evaluator would deconstruct discourses of need through a textual analysis of legislative, policy and organisational documents. In the chapter that followed, we extended this by suggesting ways in which texts of practice may be generated to be then subjected to critical scrutiny, to deconstruction for reconstruction. We suggested that evaluation is about deconstructing what come to be known as truths and generating opportunities for 'practice talk' to create alternative discourses. Thus, users and practitioners are not treated as objects from whom data are collected. Neither are their experiences and views regarded as authentic and true any more than anyone else's are. Instead, in the evaluation process, users and practitioners become active citizens engaged, with each other, in 'practice talk'.

We are left with a problem however. If there are many, everchanging truths of practice, if there is no epistemological possibility of reaching or unearthing the truth of practice through rigorous, systematic and theoretically informed empirical enquiry, then how are judgements made about what is going on in that practice and with what effects? And furthermore, do there exist some fundamental, universal standards by which we may judge whether practice is 'good', 'good enough', 'poor' or even 'corrupt'? Our task in this chapter is to answer these questions.

Interpreting data and evidence

For the sake of bringing some conceptual clarity to our analysis, we have separated out the two aspects of evaluation: generating evidence about practice and making judgements about its value. Partly this separation is an analytical device and it is important to remember that making judgements, and prioritising and being accountable to values, pervades the entire evaluative process. We have argued throughout this text that data are not external facts and truths that may be collected and understood separately from context, processes and values. Data and evidence are produced through deconstructing what has come to be known and perhaps taken-for-granted about the practice and through interpreting practice.

The process of developing evidence of practice is one of generating a 'good enough' picture of what is going on. It is a picture that portrays 'a' truth, not 'the' truth, of the practice which is helpful. It may be a picture that shows quite unexpected things about what is going on. It is also a picture that will be looked at in different ways by, and mean different things to, those involved in the practice in various capacities. It will hang alongside other pictures in the gallery of practice, both those that have been created before and maybe cherished and valued over time (some, with the new picture hanging, may be pushed into the shade, stored in the basement or thrown out) and those that are still to be drawn and fleshed out with colour and detail. That the picture created does not portray 'the' truth does not mean that it has not been developed with care to detail, tone, shading and perspective. Generating the evidence of practice will only be 'good enough' if the process is engaged in systematically and coherently with rigour. As Maynard writes in relation to feminist research:

> the issue is not so much about objectivity (with its positivistic connotations of facticity), nor of value-neutrality (and the supposed null effect of the researcher on her research), as about the soundness and reliability of feminist research. Feminist work needs to be rigorous if it is to be regarded as intellectually compelling, politically persuasive, policy-relevant and meaningful to anyone other than feminists themselves. (Maynard, 1994: 24)

So, too, evaluation must be theoretically informed and coherent, credible in policy-making arenas and political discourse, and must make sense to those outside of the immediate practice. We have stressed the importance of evaluation being close to practice and warned against external, expert managerial evaluators. But how often do practice-based evaluations look like public relations exercises?

Or how often do they read like lists of data, tables of statistics, and expected stories that have been produced in the knowledge that this is what the funders or managers want?

The process of generating evidence must be undertaken in the spirit of searching for 'the' truth but with a recognition that the task is never completed. The evidence itself must be subject to scrutiny and processes of deconstruction so that it does not form a 'regime of truth', a form of power/knowledge. But for the moment, the evidence will do. It must be as good as it can be to enable those having a stake in the practice to engage in debate as to what is going on and to what effect. The place of theories and values in this process of deconstruction and reconstruction of data and evidence cannot be overemphasised in this rational-technical world which spawns, and somewhat thrives upon, managerial evaluation. How we see the world, and ourselves, is constructed through concepts, meanings and words that we have available to us as well as through our experiences, our social position in relation to others and our values. 'We' and 'our' applies not only to those that have the task of generating data but those who provide data for the evaluation.

The process of data generation is a social, interactive one involving both evaluators and those from whom data are collected, the researchers and the researched. Holland and Ramazanoglu (1994) helpfully map out the research process putting interpretation in its place. Theories, concepts, ideas, power, values, experience and self-identity of researchers and researched interact in the processes involved in formulating and responding to questions, in producing and interpreting data, in being mindful to the meanings of silences and 'missing data', and in drawing conclusions. Differences in social class, gender, age, disability, sexuality and ethnicity interact with all of these and with the very processes of interaction and interpretation.

So experiences people have of the practice relayed

through the evaluation by users, practitioners, workers in other agencies, members of management committees, are not treated as truth but as interpretation. Experience articulated to another is lived experience with meaning and significance attached to it in an interactive process between 'researcher' and 'researched' through the use of words, concepts and theories that are available at the time. And further interpretation is involved on the part of those responsible for putting the evidence together in the processes of scrutinising data and evidence so that patterns, themes, issues, concerns and claims may be drawn out in order that judgements be made.

The theoretical analytical process of interpreting data and evidence is described by Holland and Ramazanoglu as one where

> the validity of experience is in constant tension with the limitations of experience which social sciences try to transcend. (Holland and Ramazanoglu, 1994: 129)

In social welfare, advocacy and social movements have been important in highlighting that people have a right to speak for themselves. But at the same time we need to be alert to reifying experiences, through supposedly radical practice, at the expense of developing more sensitive understandings. Reflecting upon feminist arguments to listen to the voices of women, Maynard writes:

> To begin with there is no such thing as 'raw' experience. Post-structuralist thinking clearly demonstrates that the very act of speaking about experience is to culturally and discursively constitute it. People's accounts of their lives are culturally embedded. Their descriptions are, at the same time, a construction of the events that occurred, together with an interpretation of them. (Maynard, 1994: 23)

The task of those involved in the evaluation is to take account of ways in which experience is constructed and recounted, not to unearth real experience but to ensure that a 'good enough' picture emerges which enables those involved in the practice to be evaluative.

The responsibilities of the evaluator

So far we have framed our words to avoid too much reference to 'the evaluator'. We opened Chapter 3 with illustrative experiences of evaluations that have produced much scepticism and ambivalence towards evaluators, particularly on the part of practitioners in social welfare. We have been concerned not to assign too much power to evaluators. We also have suggested that while everyone involved in the practice should have a right to contribute to its evaluation, the practitioner has a responsibility to do so and to ensure that no-one is marginalised in this process.

In moving from total reliance upon the measurement of practice to produce the truth, evaluators have assumed more and more responsibility for making judgements about effectiveness. Guba and Lincoln have pointed out that we, including evaluators, are right to be cautious when

> the evaluator assumed the role of judge, while retaining the earlier technical descriptive functions as well. (Guba and Lincoln, 1989: 30)

They expose a number of problems with this position:

> First, it required that the objectives themselves be taken as problematic; goals no less than performance were to be subject to evaluation. . . . Further, judgement requires standards against which the judgement can be made. But the inclusion of standards that must, by definition of the genre, be value-laden into a scientific and putatively value-free enterprise such as evaluation, was repugnant to most evaluators. Finally, if there is to be judgement, there must be a judge. Evaluators did

> not feel competent to act in that capacity, felt it presumptuous to do so, and feared the political vulnerability to which it exposed them. Nevertheless, they were urged to accept that obligation, largely on the ground that, among all possible judge candidates, the evaluators were without doubt the most objective. (Guba and Lincoln, 1989: 30)

These writers proceed by suggesting that 'evaluators soon rose to the challenge' (Guba and Lincoln, 1989: 30) so that judgement became integral to evaluation with, more or less explicitly, the evaluator becoming the judge.

In recognising the place of judgement-making and interpretation throughout the evaluation process, it is right that we guard against investing too much authority in the expert evaluator. And yet there are skills and scholarship involved in social science and in using the social sciences to 'transcend experience'. These can be made accessible (as in Everitt and Gibson, 1994, for example); but also, social scientists, in engaging in evaluations with those involved in practice, must become accountable. Such accountability is necessary throughout the evaluation process because the process is not technical: it is political. House points out that:

> Philosophically, evaluators ceased believing that their discipline was value-free. Politically, they saw that evaluation had political effects. Their early attempts to find definitive solutions to social problems proved to be a disappointing venture. Rather, the concepts of evaluation that evolved reflected the change from consensus to pluralism that was occurring in the larger society. (House, 1993: viii)

Making visible evaluation as a political process should not diminish it as a process which requires skilful and theoretically informed data generation, analytical and interpretation methods. On the contrary, that evaluation is political emphasises the need for rigour and coherence, and this

> involves being clear about one's theoretical assumptions, the nature of the research process, the criteria against which 'good' knowledge can be judged and the strategies used for interpretation and analysis. In feminist work the suggestion is that all these things are made available for scrutiny, comment and (re)negotiation, as part of the process through which standards are evaluated and judged. (Maynard, 1994: 25)

Holland and Ramazanoglu (1994) in their account of researching young women's sexuality reflect on ways in which the data generated through interviews with young women may be interpreted in quite different ways and thus lead to different policy recommendations. They write though that not 'all interpretations are equally valid'. To adopt such

> a relativist position on policy offers freedom to masculinist researchers or those on the 'new right' to suggest further constraints on women's lives. Distinguishing between policies is always a matter both of values and of the power of the theory used. (Holland and Ramazanoglu, 1994: 133)

For these researchers, the guide in prioritising some interpretations of the data over others is to contemplate 'for whom' the policies are intended. For them and their colleagues, their research is intended to contribute to policy aimed at 'empowering young women to take more control of their sexual safety' (Holland and Ramazanoglu, 1994: 133).

In according some in the practice with particular responsibilities for the evaluation, be they practitioners or evaluators (which may be necessary bearing in mind people's time, expertise and resources), it is important that these responsibilities are undertaken in accountable ways. But to what or whom should the practitioner or evaluator be responsible? Everitt and Gibson (1994), in mapping out an approach to researching in the voluntary sector, propose that researchers be accountable to the intended beneficiaries of voluntary projects. This may mean, in many cases, making the research meaningful to those who have responsibility to act on behalf of intended beneficiaries, such as practitioners, members of management committees, local authority personnel and elected members. So, as the research team of which Holland and Ramaanoglu are members tries to ensure accountability to young women, evaluators in social welfare organisations should be accountable to users, older people attending day centres, young people in care, and many more who may otherwise suffer from 'poor' or even 'corrupt' practice.

As well as being accountable to young women, the accountability described by Holland and Ramazanoglu contains within it a theoretical and value perspective about women, autonomy and empowerment in a dangerous society. It is not enough to profess accountability to intended beneficiaries of social welfare organisations albeit that this is a vast improvement upon evaluators having too much regard for keeping in with those who have the power to fund and commission evaluations – and provide further means of earning income. Meaningful accountability requires a commitment to values, an accountability to standards.

It is interesting to reflect that so little attention has been paid to values in evaluation and yet they are so central. Connor (1993) suggests that this is generally so in the humanities and social sciences where there has been more concern with issues of meaning and interpretation than with values and judgements. He illustrates his argument by referring to the field of education where a host of rapid changes in government policy and funding for schools, and adult and higher education, amount to

> a rejection of the concept of an evaluative discipline in favour of a positivist and instrumentalist model of education as training, a model which was itself derived from a narrowly idealised version of scientific and technical education,

> in which facts, knowledge and interpretation have an ascendancy over values and the processes of value-judgement. (Connor, 1993: 33)

A similar analysis could be made of social work and social welfare as policies and funding turn to rule-books, procedures and outputs. Evaluation of the managerial rational-technical kind has acted as a discipline contributing to the control and marginalisation of debates about values driving values

> into the critical unconscious, where they continue to exercise force but without being available for analytic scrutiny. (Connor, 1993: 34)

In building judgement-making into evaluation we are attempting to firmly locate it in the political arena of public debate where it rightly belongs.

Values, standards and the notion of the good

> Value is inescapable. This is not to be taken as a claim for the objective existence or categorical force of any values or imperatives in particular; but rather as a claim that the processes of estimating, ascribing, modifying, affirming and even denying value, in short, the processes of evaluation, can never be avoided. (Connor, 1993: 31)

Postmodernist theory, in its analysis of 'regimes of truth' and the relationship between knowledge and power rightly makes us tentative about proposing that there are essential values which should guide judgement-making and interpretation processes in evaluation. In a patriarchal society divided by race, social class, disability, age and sexuality we are only too aware of the inherent danger to people's freedom and equality in making a case for adherence to certain values. The predominant values of our society, maintained and strengthened through a myriad of processes and actions, have served to render, in systematic ways, some people vulnerable and fearful with little access to resources to enable them to live a full and flourishing life: women, older people, Black people, disabled men and women, young people without work, children in abusive homes.

The early 1990s has witnessed a host of values, particularly 'family' values, telling us how we should or should not live our lives. Some people – single mothers, young homeless people, 'new age' travellers – are picked off and treated as 'other', categorised as feckless and judged to be not living up to the central values of the moral majority of our society. And this from a government guilty not only of overseeing increasing inequality but of engaging in or condoning corrupt practices in public life. Values must be treated with care, constantly appraised for the ways in which they can become absolute 'regimes of truth', significant parts of discourses that maintain power relations in an unequal society.

In attempts to reinstate the responsibilities social workers have for theorising and the making of moral judgements, some writers have turned to Aristotelian thinking about the 'good'. Whan (1986), for example, finds the notion of phronesis, or prudence, useful in referring to moral knowledge. Aristotle distinguishes this from episteme, scientific knowledge and from techne, technical skill. Whan argues that phronesis is the form of knowledge most appropriate for social work involving deliberating, reflecting, making judgements and choosing to act in the direction of the 'good'. This form of knowing cannot be taken from procedural manuals, rather it involves making moral judgements, being enquiring and adopting a less certain approach to both the ends and means of practice. It entails a moral engagement with practice, a process of exploring through dialogue the meaning of practice for all involved and then being able to make judgements to move that practice in the direction of the 'good'. Jeffs and Smith (1990) suggest that the notion of direction

> involves having a personal but shared idea of the 'good': some notion of what makes for human flourishing and well-being. (Jeffs and Smith, 1990: 17)

Everitt *et al.* (1992) use this idea of 'direction' in arguing that this forms a yardstick against which judgements between competing views may be made, and indeed should be made as part of professional responsibility.

The idea of 'the direction of the good' rather than 'the good' is useful in alerting us to the dangers of absolute notions of good. Bertrand Russell (1974) points out, for example, that the Aristotelian 'good' quite definitely can be understood as a product of the society in which he lived and thus a 'regime of truth' to maintain existing unequal power relations. We can see from this example how important it is to resist absolute values and to subject prevailing values to scrutiny to reveal in whose interests they operate, and who loses.

> Aristotle's opinions on moral questions are such as were conventional in his day. On some points they differ from those of our time, chiefly where some form of aristocracy comes in. We think that human beings, at least in ethical theory, all have equal rights, and that justice involves equality; Aristotle thinks that justice involves, not equality, but right proportion, which is only sometimes equality. (Russell, 1974: 186)

Thus, Aristotle argues that slaves to masters, sons to fathers, wives to husbands, should all respect the superiority of the more powerful!

Russell's own values, those of benevolence and regard for others, have too to be treated with caution. Foucault has very clearly exposed the ways in which disciplinary regimes such as social work act as powerful mechanisms of surveillance and social control through their doing good unto others. Foucault and other commentators have remarked on the paradoxical nature of humanist caring.

> In determining the needs and rights of citizens, humanists are said to install new and extended patterns of surveillance and control which unavoidably limit the freedom of the individual. For example, acceptance of the principle that the state is responsible for caring for individuals who are in distress demands precise delineation of the conditions in which care is approved or withheld. Individuals are required to be examined in order to ascertain if their needs are 'real' or 'false', and whether their claims on state resources are 'deserving' or 'undeserving'. Moreover, social workers must obey an officially approved protocol of behaviour in the administration of care. (Rojek, Peacock and Collins, 1988: 115)

Feminist writers and criminologists have shown ways in which the integral relationship between care and control in social work has been particularly powerful in maintaining gender roles, ensuring that young women behave as good girls and women, conform to what is expected of them as wives, mothers and daughters (Hudson, 1989; Hooper, 1992). Fox (1993) writes about the ways in which people are constructed through discourses of health-talk to behave, think and think of themselves as patients dependent upon the power, knowledge and decisions of professionals.

So we are left with values being essential to evaluation but being dangerous should any particular value come to be regarded as essential or fundamental. As Parton notes:

> The problem is we cannot evaluate according to any absolute standard of progress. While trying to differentiate between acceptable and unacceptable practices and positions we must recognise that this is always necessarily contentious and incomplete. (Parton, 1994a: 110)

Values must be constantly scrutinised and deconstructed. We must strive for making judgements in the direction of the 'good', just as we must strive for 'truth', but we must be tentative about the status of 'a value' and 'the truth'.

> The structure of value is therefore paradoxical, involving the simultaneous desire and necessity to affirm unconditional values and the desire and necessity of subjecting such values to continuous, corrosive scrutiny. (Connor, 1993: 38)

Despite the difficulty with values it is vital that values are returned to professional practice and that practitioners are able to promote 'good' and 'good enough' practice while at the same time having no hesitation in exposing 'poor' or even 'corrupt' practice. Evaluation has to be developed to enable social welfare organisations to be evaluative and to move practice in the direction of the 'good', to address inequality and power relations and work towards ensuring that all people are able to flourish as active citizens. In problematising the 'truth', postmodernist thinking necessitates our being able to make judgements within contexts of always incomplete knowledge. Judgements about 'good' practice are in the end political judgements. They are not decisions based on an uncontested, universally agreed truth. Recognising this removes decision-making about 'good' practice, 'poor' and 'corrupt' practice, from the technical agenda, away from the control, and possibly cover-up, of experts, into the political arena. As Parton notes:

> One consequence of the undermining of universal science, knowledge and truth, is that all views, interests and arguments are potentially valid – it relocates politics as central to everyday life. (Parton, 1994b: 28)

Democracy and rights in evaluation

Problematising the truth and seeing the need to deconstruct values does not obviate the need for values and for a political project. The very postmodernist project is driven by theories of power and the integral relationship between power and knowledge. The methodology of deconstruction is informed by the theories having as their purpose the constant process of making truth claims, and the ways in which they act powerfully to maintain inequalities visible and subject to critical scrutiny.

Fraser, having made an extremely cogent argument for

> shifting the focus of inquiry from needs to discourses about needs, from the distribution of need satisfactions to the 'politics of need interpretation' (Fraser, 1989: 292)

concludes with

> the question whether and how it is possible to distinguish better from worse interpretations of people's needs. (Fraser, 1989: 311)

Her answer to this crucial question is clear and unequivocal and is central to this chapter on judgement-making:

> we can distinguish better from worse interpretations of people's needs. To say that needs are culturally constructed and discursively interpreted is not to say that any need interpretation is as good as any other. On the contrary, it is to underline the importance of an account of interpretive justification. (Fraser, 1989: 311–12)

It may be useful to think of evaluation as 'accounts of interpretive justification' rather than as measurement of performance against predetermined indicators or measurement of outputs and correlations between outputs and outcomes. Fraser continues her argument by outlining two quite separate considerations in such 'accounts of interpretive justification':

- first, there are procedural considerations concerning the social processes by which various competing need interpretations are generated . . . the best need interpretations are those reached by means of communicative processes that most closely approximate ideals of democracy, equality and fairness (Fraser, 1989: 312).
- consequentialist considerations are also relevant in justifying need interpretations. These considerations involve comparing alternative distributive outcomes of rival interpretations. . . . consequentialist considerations dictate that, all other things being equal, the best need interpretations are those that do not disadvantage some groups of people vis-a-vis others (Fraser, 1989: 312).

Thus, it is imperative that social welfare practice (including programmes, policies and projects) is continuously evaluated and is subject to in-depth serial evaluations to ensure that:

- practice is developed and engaged in through democratic and fair processes having equality as its underpinning value and its goal;
- practice responds to needs negotiated through democratic and fair processes of equality;
- practice has the effect of bringing about equality enabling all people, irrespective of their sex, ethnicity, age, economic position, social class and disability, to flourish and enjoy human well-being.

Practice is judged to be 'good' if it meets these criteria. Knowing that power is always present cautions against thinking in terms of the 'good', preferring to think of the state of democracy, fairness and equality as becoming, judging practice for its working in the direction of the 'good'. Practice is 'good enough' if it can be seen as working in the direction of the 'good', i.e. in working towards the implementation of democratic, fair and equal processes to bring about equality. Practice is 'poor' if it makes no attempt to meet the criteria of democracy, fairness and equality. It is 'corrupt' if it is anti-democratic, autocratic, unfair and if it treats those that it is there to serve as though they are 'other', not equal to 'us'.

These same values are adopted by Biehal and colleagues in their work on rights and social work (Biehal *et al.*, 1992). They warn against the disempowering effects of

> defining people's needs for them, making decisions on their behalf and denying them responsibility through the exercise of professional discretion, current practice may serve as a barrier to entitlement to welfare. (Biehal *et al.*, 1992: 110)

They argue that decisions about need should be a matter for negotiation rather than subject to supposedly objective analysis undertaken technically by the practitioner. Users should be involved in all aspects of service design, planning, delivery, and evaluation. They acknowledge that 'a statement of rights cannot guarantee changes in professional practice' (Biehal *et al.*, 1992: 112) but propose that nevertheless it can be valuable, for three reasons:

- it sets out for public scrutiny the agency philosophy governing service . . .
- it sets some targets (albeit procedural ones) for practice and clarifies the standards that social workers are expected to achieve . . .
- it provides an external reference point for the exchanges between workers and clients. (Biehal *et al.*, 1992: 113)

People should not only be involved in the evaluation of services, in making judgements as to whether social work is practising in the direction of the 'good'. They

> should have the right to expect that their evaluation of service will be regarded as an important element in future service planning. (Biehal *et al.*, 1992: 125)

User involvement in evaluation means their being fully informed, being confident to speak on their terms, being respected as subjects in their own right, being 'positively assisted in presenting their views' (Biehal *et al.*, 1992: 123), being in a position to tell 'rival stories' (Fox, 1993: 9). This is quite a different approach from being asked to express views within a framework set by the organisation and evaluator.

We can now answer the question posed by Guba and Lincoln: who should be the judges? It is quite clear that it is inappropriate for evaluators alone to be the ones to make judgements about the value of practice. Their task is to provide evidence and to facilitate the process of judgement-making informed by this evidence. So, too, it is not appropriate for practitioners alone to be judges of their own practice. It is their responsibility to ensure that these judgements are made through democratic processes.

Democracy is central to evaluation in two ways:

- first, the purpose of evaluation is to ensure that practice is 'good', democratic, fair and equal, or is developing in the direction of the 'good';
- second, the process of evaluation can contribute to practice being 'good' or developing in the direction of the 'good' by democratising ways in which needs come to be understood and responses to these needs decided upon and implemented.

Evaluation may become a process through which all those involved in social welfare practice are able to not only articulate their experiences but also understand them and politicise them. In this way, through its process as well as its product, evaluation may contribute to social change in the direction of the 'good'. Care needs to be taken to develop ways to ensure that all have equal opportunity 'to create the texts of practice' (Freire, 1972). This requires an understanding and analysis of ways in which people's subjectivity is constructed through discourses. It requires the use of imaginative methods to provide people with opportunities to tell 'rival stories', to develop alternative discourses. Fox, for example, drawing upon women's approaches to writing about their lives within the feminist movement, suggests this as one way to create

> a forum for positive agency: space to act in a world where it is more usual to be the subject of writing. Writing's relative permanence paradoxically makes it less permanent – able to be changed, rubbed out, refined or trashed. Writing enables reflection: it can be returned to, contextualised, reread. (Fox, 1993: 109)

Practitioners in social welfare have at their disposal a myriad of ways to facilitate the articulation and reflection upon experience by people, including those who may not always have the language skills to engage in writing and conversation. Thomson points out that practitioners

> are in daily contact with service users. That contact at its best can be a fruitful dialogue and sow the seeds for a new partnership between service providers and users. (Thomson, 1992: 148–9)

Whittaker (1994) for example, describes an evaluation in which learning-disabled people themselves evaluated residential services for seven people moving from hospital into two group homes. Howe, too, emphasises the democratic requirements of decision-making since 'understanding is no longer a mode of knowing, but a dialogical activity' (Howe, 1994: 525):

> If there are no privileged perspectives, no centres of truth, no absolute authorities in matters of taste and judgement, then all truths are working truths and relative truths. The

full participation of those involved in decisions about what is going on and what should be done is the only way to define non-oppressive, culturally pertinent truths and working, practical judgements. (Howe, 1994: 525)

Case example

As part of the arts project in elderly persons' homes, a small group of older people from one home went to the pottery sessions together. They discussed possible projects with the potter, wanting to do something together and make something that they would be able to take 'back home' with them. Their discussions raised all kinds of issues such as what would happen to the results of their work in the tidiness of the residential home, what could they do that they would feel ownership of but at the same time could be shared in the home. Eventually the idea of a bird-bath emerged. Through talking about the place of pottery in the home, they realised that not only did the home have a feeling of not belonging to them, but this was even more the case with the garden. The grounds around the home were designed with lawn-mowing and car-parking in mind. There was no corner to sit in. Residents rarely went outside of the home except on those very hot days when chairs would be placed immediately by the front door, in a row looking out on to the cars parked and beyond them to the road. Making a bird-bath would be something they could do together, something they could take back with them and, through it, tell a 'rival story' and make a corner of the garden theirs. There is now an attractive corner of the garden where people sit together, no doubt telling 'rival stories'. (Everitt, 1994)

Given that experience is constructed through discourses and social processes, as well as facilitating the articulation and understanding of experience it is vital that evaluation engages in

'challenging methods', by which we mean ways of conducting research which not only create knowledge, but are designed to question oppressive attitudes and behaviour . . . to encourage within the research process a questioning in the participants of their suppositions. (Kelly, Burton and Regan, 1994: 38–9)

9

Conclusion

We shall attempt now to stand back a little from our text. We have argued that evaluators themselves should not be the sole arbiters or judges of practice. They have a responsibility to generate evidence of the 'truths' of practice as competently as they possibly can. Evaluators should also be accountable for the evidence they provide and the appraisals they generate. Critical evaluators should participate with as many stakeholders as possible in jointly reaching judgements about the value of an activity, programme or policy. Likewise, they should work developmentally in mutually negotiated change processes. Criteria for evaluating whether practice is 'good', 'good enough', 'poor' or 'corrupt' are not plucked from the air. Nor are they chosen 'top down' or arbitrarily. These criteria are grounded in the realities of political economy and constructed through value positions, which include those of democracy, justice, equality and anti-oppression.

The Welfare State is changing. Research alerts us to the need to research change, and one aspect that surely demands research and evaluation is the move away from democracy and democratic processes in the planning and management of service delivery. We cannot take the Welfare State for granted. We need to research and evaluate the minutiae of policies, procedures and processes, and to engage in evaluation for 'good' practice.

Needs

The conceptual framework of needs-discourses in Chapter 6 helped us to explore some of the ways in which needs are politically contested and used as levers in social policy implementation. Accordingly, we were able to analyse some of the needs-discourses and their consequences in children's and community care legislation. Drawing upon Fraser's work (1989) alerts us to ways in which needs are constructed through languages and processes. At the same time, needs do exist, and, through research, patterns of need are unfurled from which we are able to deduce the prevalence and pervasiveness of structural inequalities. There are some postmodernists who argue that there is a reality beyond and outside the languages and processes that construct it. Our approach (and that of realists within postmodernism, such as Layder, 1993), also recognises that there is a reality not constructed merely through processes, practices and words. It is this reality, interpreted as social structure, that in complex ways relates to the lives people lead, their needs and the views they have of themselves and the social world. Postmodernist thinking alerts us to the complexity of the relationship between individuals' thoughts and actions and social structure – a relationship more complex than one of determinism and cause. Through research, patterns of social relations and social actions may be discovered from which social structures may be deduced. So, for example, Walby (1990) suggests that while patriarchy cannot be found through research, patterns of gender inequality can be, through which patriarchy as social structure may be deduced.

The debate about the nature of needs and their satisfactions (especially through the Welfare State) continues to wage unabated. As we have made claims to make our values explicit, some of the issues raised for us in this literature will be addressed, however briefly.

- *Needs, rights and welfare*

Plant *et al.* (1980) argue that the recognition and satisfaction of need marks the welfare function of the modern state from its other functions. The identification of basic needs generates moral obligations for these to be met: needs for survival and personal autonomy, freedom from arbitrary interest, ill-health and ignorance. Members of any society have a duty to create social systems that will satisfy these needs as well as possible. For Plant *et al.* the general concept of human need is not relative even though there will be cultural variations and it is important to recognise and respect difference and diversity. The needy have moral claims on those better off and this is the moral basis of welfare provision. Furthermore, the relationship between needs and rights is central to the problem of stigma for the users of welfare services.

- *Needs, vulnerability and social protection*

Goodin (1985) argues that we all acknowledge special responsibilities to family, friends, clients and compatriots, etc. These special responsibilities are relatively strong moral claims. The moral basis of these special responsibilities is traditionally analysed in terms of self-assumed obligations, so that we voluntarily commit ourselves to only a limited range of people (Finch, 1989). However, it is the vulnerability of the beneficiary rather than the benefactor's voluntary commitment which generates these special responsibilities. Thus, social protection becomes a very broad responsibility operating at many levels: interpersonal, international, intergenerational and environmental. Some vulnerabilities are natural, inevitable and immutable; others are created, shaped or sustained by current social arrangements.

> Whilst we should always strive to protect the vulnerable, we should also strive to reduce the latter sort of vulnerabilities

> in so far as they render the vulnerable liable to exploitation. (Goodin, 1985: xi).

This argument recognises a much more extensive network of obligations and moral claims than has been traditionally acknowledged.

- *Needs and welfare*

Ware and Goodin (1990) argue that state welfare meets needs according to contrasting principles: redistributionist, communitarian and social citizenship. Services are provided both to help those defined to be in need and to prevent people falling into need. In Britain since the Poor Law, there has been universal, though limited, coverage for all those who fit the current definition of need. In Germany, welfare is met through state-directed insurance linked to employment and contributions; coverage is fixed by contributions not 'needs'. In Scandinavia, welfare is based on a social citizenship, rights model.

> The New Right may have placed issues on the agenda of welfare politics that had been absent in the consensual mid-century years, but the western state is likely to remain what it became during the course of the twentieth century – the main institution responding to need in western society. (Ware and Goodin, 1990: 10)

This is confirmed in a major research project which indicates that the Welfare State in Britain has been surprisingly robust since 1974 (Hills *et al.*, 1993).

- *A theory of human need*

Doyal and Gough (1991) eschew subjectivist and relativist (or interpretivist) approaches to human needs in their argument that all humans have basic needs in common which cannot be reduced to individual cultural preferences.

Health and autonomy are essential preconditions for participation in social life and thus constitute objective and universal needs. The optimal satisfaction of these needs is the fundamental human right of all individuals. These authors develop cross-cultural indicators of need satisfaction and use these to measure and compare levels of human welfare throughout the world. They identify a dual strategy which optimises need satisfaction and recognises the economic importance of the market and central planning plus the political importance of state intervention and a flourishing democracy. They radically redraw the contours of debates about human needs and the obligations on civil society to satisfy these. They develop some universal laws of social life and are developmental in their commitment to social change and their explicit avowal of social democratic and socialist principles.

These texts remind us that the definition of universal and objective needs and the role of welfare states in satisfying these is still on the moral and political agenda. The fact that there are many vulnerable people in our society who need protection makes moral claims upon us whether we choose to act on these or not; their vulnerability generates responsibilities for us. The debates about needs and rights will continue and it is always important to identify the values which underpin and legitimate our social arrangements, including social policy and social welfare. This literature thus provides a context within which the purposes of evaluation are enshrined. When we ask questions about the value of an activity, a policy, a programme or a project, we are also asking questions about needs, vulnerability and social protection in welfare states.

Critical theory

Social science was born as critical theory. Its purpose and intention was to address the major problems and issues in western industrialising societies. Sometimes it lost its way in this respect with the rise and fall of new paradigms. However, viewed historically the best literature and research in the social sciences has always been 'critical'.

Fay describes what he means by critical social science:

> The critical model is 'critical'... in that it sees theories as analyses of a social situation in terms of those features of it which can be altered in order to eliminate certain frustrations which members in it are experiencing, and its method of testing the truth of a social scientific theory consists partially of ascertaining the theory's practical relevance in leading to the satisfaction of human needs and purposes. (Fay, 1975: 92)

He outlines the features of critical social science thus:

- it accepts the necessity of interpretative categories in social science;
- it is aware that many actions people perform are constructed by social conditions and through social processes, and that people are thus objectified and their agency limited. It, therefore, seeks to uncover those systems of social relationships (i.e. structural) which construct the actions of individuals, including the unanticipated though not accidental consequences of these actions;
- it gives explicit recognition to the interconnections between social theory and social practice.

The social practices described by Fay include: articulating the grievances of oppressed groups; ideology critique; involving oppressed actors in the process through the educational role of social theory; constant critical interchange between policy experts and the actors affected by their decisions.

> A critical social theory is itself a catalytic agent of change within the complex of social life which it analyses. (Fay, 1975: 110)

Finally, the 'intimate connection . . . between the ideas that we have and the sort of life that we lead' (Fay, 1975: 11) shapes the ways in which to conduct social inquiry. Evaluators should not be judges. They need to be accountable, to engage in dialogue and to democratise their work.

Writing twelve years later, Fay reaches a very humble conclusion:

> I no longer think critical social science holds the key to redeeming our social and political life. But I do think that, suitably amended and limited in aspiration, it can provide an important source of social understanding and a much-needed impetus for the social and political changes which will have to take place if human life is to continue. (Fay, 1987: ix])

All seekers after truth believe that the truth will set them free (Bailey, 1980). Those involved in evaluation are simultaneously seekers after truth while realising in their every endeavour that truth is an illusion and something to which they can only ever approximate. Learning and knowledge-building can be (and should be) very humbling experiences.

Social work, social welfare and 'the good'

We sometimes think, and it is frequently asserted, that one of Thatcher's legacies is the disappearance of 'good' social work and social welfare as we have known it. The legalism in the 1989 Children Act, the monetarism in the 1990 NHS and Community Care Act and the retributivism in criminal justice which has impacted upon probation service objectives are cited as undermining welfare policies and practices. Voluntary agencies have been criticised for acting like pressure groups and being 'too political', and many of them are constrained by service level agreements and driven by outputs. It can readily be seen that performance measurement finds a place in these social transformations and is becoming a dominant mode of evaluation, or control, in the public sector.

However, this tale is far too simple. Social work and social welfare in every age have had to address the political economy of the era (Hardiker and Barker, 1991; Hardiker, 1994c). Political economy has been brought into sharp relief ever since the economic crises of the mid-1970s. Social work does not stand on its own outside of the political, legal, economic and social institutions which legitimate it and shape its values and objectives (Hardiker, Exton and Barker, 1991b, 1991c). Accordingly, social work purposes and processes have to take into account contemporary rules of evidence, changing policies, priority groupings and targeting; parental responsibilities and the rights of extended kin, etc. But 'good' practice in social work and social welfare has survived. During periods of rapid social change, it is often easier to see discontinuities rather than continuities, contradictions rather than overlaps. We can make the same point in respect of social work and social welfare, and this behoves us to balance our evidence very carefully. Is the kernel of welfare practices still that of enabling adaptations between people and their environments and representing and restoring the humanity and subjectivity of people in distress or need so that they can become members participating in civil society (Payne, 1991)?

Social workers and their managers do not, of course,

always succeed in achieving these purposes. And, as Mary Richmond (1917) said, social workers have a duty and responsibility to bear witness to social casualties wherever they may find them. There is evidence that practice in the direction of the 'good' is still alive in British welfare institutions as its practitioners implement new legislation. Hardiker and Barker for example (1994a) analysed ways in which social work processes enabled workers to practise with vulnerable families in complex and volatile situations so that difficulties were resolved and children rehabilitated safely home.

The same social work processes are in evidence in needs-led assessments and care packages for vulnerable adults under the new community care arrangements (Hardiker and Barker, 1994b). Counselling and social care planning are still in evidence as elderly people are enabled to relinquish their homes, parents are enabled to use respite facilities for their children, the needs of disabled people are addressed through advocacy schemes and Independent Living Fund arrangements, and adults with long-term mental health difficulties plus their parents are supported as they move to live independently from one another. Classical groupwork methods find their place in work with high-risk offenders placed under probation orders with conditions (Willis, 1991). Community development approaches are still much in evidence in many voluntary projects (Mayo, 1994). Thus, there are still continuities in social welfare practice even though there have been great changes in political economy.

The purpose and focus of critical evaluation

Critical evaluation uses conceptual frameworks outlined in critical theory. It combines analyses of power at structural, interpersonal and personal levels with an understanding of both how subjectivity is constructed and how human agency is strengthened. This is done in the interests of good practice: unpacking and interrogating those features of the social milieu which can be altered in order to eliminate or reduce people's deprivations, frustrations and, yes, needs. Accordingly, critical evaluation explores the structures and processes through which subjectivities are shaped and maintained: included in these are those which render some powerful and others not.

The dimensions to be addressed in a critical evaluation include:

- An examination of the historical and socio-political contexts of the policies and practices being evaluated. We have attempted to do this by examining the legislative, social policy, professional and organisational underpinnings through which the practices described were constructed: children's, community care and probation services; community development, education and arts projects. These features of the context are not static backcloths for the practice stage but are continually constructed and negotiated through powerful social relations during the practice process.
- Forms of oppression are addressed because thereby the ways in which certain practices and understandings are constructed are revealed. In social welfare, many users of services are extremely disadvantaged: their social class, place in the labour market, their gender, ethnicity, age, disabilities, sexual orientation, construct many needs for them: deprivation, discrimination, exclusion, low esteem and stigma. Services set up to address these needs may further compound their disadvantages if they are buttressed by discriminatory policies and practices. Any evaluation must address ways in which these oppressive practices and their consequences are played out and must purposefully strive towards anti-oppressive practices and equality.
- Ways in which social welfare practices become routinised

need to be addressed. This can be attempted by deconstructing commonly accepted ways of doing things and understandings so that they are not taken-for-granted. They are, thus, also made available for explicit scrutiny, critique and appraisal. Many of the methodologies we have developed render implicit practices explicit; accordingly, our research interviews in the welfare field themselves become a mode of supervision and evaluation. The discourse analyses we have undertaken are also a means of deconstructing taken-for-granted *modus operandi.*

- Values take centre stage in critical evaluation and we have made some claims to theories of democracy, social justice, rights and universal needs to guide us. Do needs discourses serve to residualise services for children and adults under new legislation? Do social pedagogic ones succeed in consciousness-raising, democratising powerful relationships and increasing access to valued services?
- We are for ever in danger of making rhetorical claims as we say that our modes of evaluation commit us to promoting change. Who are we to say that policies and practices need changing? These claims can only ever even begin to be justified if we adopt certain methodological and democratic approaches in critical evaluations.

The methodological approaches of critical evaluation include:

- Capturing people's understandings of what a policy or programme does, with what effects, for whom. We shall not achieve this by examining structural variables or subjective interpretations exclusively. We have to triangulate, within the limits of our resources, so that we can grasp the impact which the authoritative intentions of policy-makers have on practitioners and users and vice versa.

- We have to theorise and collect data about the ways social inequalities shape people's understandings and misunderstandings of welfare policies and practices. We must avoid the essentialist trap of treating social class, age, ethnicity, gender, disability, sexual orientation as deviant categories. Many users of welfare services are indeed multiply disadvantaged given the vulnerable circumstances of their lives. We must listen to them and provide opportunity for them to act. We must interrogate the interstices which brought them to this place. We must also cut through the social constructs of those who are paid to serve them.
- The critical evaluator engages in a process of emancipatory dialogue, thinking and practising otherwise. Some of our own evaluations have been more dialogical than others. We have not always even succeeded in gaining users' perspectives on projects and practices. When this happens we have to supplement our understandings from secondary sources and be dialogical too about the interpretations conveyed there. We should, for example, expect there to be discrepancies, even conflicts, between users, carers, practitioners and managers in many welfare settings.
- Praxis means that we are responsible for developing strategies for policy and change revealed as necessary through the evaluation process. This is easier said than done and we have often only made very modest inroads into this requirement for critical evaluation. Critical evaluators should contribute to these processes; they are not the sole arbiters or judges in praxis.
- None of us is fully aware of the social forces which shape our understandings and we have to try to grasp some of these without falling into crude determinism. Our excursion into discourse analysis illustrated the need for this. Facts do not speak for themselves and the ideologies underlying legislation have to be interrogated: structurally, interpretively and textually.

- Both qualitative and quantitative approaches can be put to the service of critical evaluation. They can each address the different levels of analysis to be excavated and also complement and supplement the findings of the other (Brannen, 1992).
- Values should not be controlled, nor should we attempt to eliminate them, but it is very difficult to be explicit about our values. Perhaps placing value positions on the agenda of every evaluation is a starting point. The race for social justice, equality and democracy certainly has still to be run.

Evaluating for good practice

In Chapter 5, we listed some tests for critical evaluation. We reproduce these here and ask the reader to reflect upon the ways in which we have approximated to our own criteria for critical evaluation in this book.

- The importance of moral debate; everyone, irrespective of power and status, has the right to legitimate opinions. Critical evaluation involves a process of debate and emancipatory dialogue with ourselves and others. Have we made a coherent theoretical and methodological argument for evaluation facilitating the process of moral debate by all involved in practice?
- Scepticism of technical, rational modes of practice. Does our scepticism and concern about rational-technical managerial evaluation contradict or cohere with our belief in systematic research and the reality, quite separate from individual subjectivity and language, of social structures, power, inequality and oppression?
- The recognition of power, powerlessness and empowerment. Have we still been too tokenistic, rhetorical and apologetic about this? Have we said anything convincing about ways in which our analyses of power

and powerlessness can facilitate the process of change stemming from and within critical evaluation? Has our work had or will it have any purchase on the empowerment of users of welfare services?

- Paying attention to the fundamental purpose of the organisation and being cautious about becoming diverted into demonstrating productivity. Have our political economy and policy and organisational analyses been 'good enough'? Has our critique of performance measurement and positivist approaches to effectiveness evaluation been sufficiently balanced, incisive and critical?
- Encouragement of openness, questioning, complaints and criticisms from outside and within the organisation. Have we provided convincing evidence of this in our examples? Have we developed an approach to evaluation that will serve to democratise organisations and practices?
- The removal of 'otherness' that may be attributed to those lower in the hierarchy, to users and to those relatively powerless in the community. Does our approach to critical evaluation provide safeguards so that users of welfare services are not pathologised or described as objects rather than subjects and human agents (Ryan, 1971)? Does it help to ensure that people in disadvantaged circumstances are never patronised? Could it be used to empower front-line practitioners and administrative staff?

We now have a responsibility to engage in further evaluations which are more thoroughly critical than some of our examples in this book. We shall not achieve the truth, but attempt to reveal the ways in which different truths are produced. This will mean addressing also the ways in which academic and professional disciplines manage the production of truth.

There is not one truth to be revealed but many truths

and perspectives articulated, suppressed, negotiated, compromised through discourses, through processes of power and powerlessness.

Such a stance requires the making of moral decisions, engaging with others in judging whether practices are 'good', 'good enough', 'poor' or 'corrupt'.

Annotated Bibliography

from Everitt, A. and Gibson, A. (1994) *Making it Work: Researching in the Voluntary Sector*, Wivenhoe, Essex, Association for Research in the Voluntary and Community Sector.

RESEARCH METHODS TEXTS

Bell, J. (1993) *Doing Your Research Project: A Guide for First-Time Researchers in Education and Social Science*, Milton Keynes, Open University Press.
This very readable and understandable text follows through the research process: considering alternative approaches to research, planning the project; reviewing the literature; keeping records and notes; getting access to information; collecting information from documentary sources, through questionnaires, interviews, diaries, and from observation; analysing information and writing-up. It is written for Open University students, particularly for those following education courses, although it is more broadly relevant for those working in the broad field of social welfare. It is particularly designed for dissertation writers, i.e. those conducting research over a period of a few months, often part-time.

Dunsire, A. and Williams, L. (1991) *How to Do Social Research*, London, Collins-Educational.
Written for A-level sociology students, this is a very accessible guide to the main social research methods. The first part focuses on understanding and evaluating social research: research through observation; social surveys; informal interviews; secondary data; using more than one method at a time. It presents summaries of pieces of research illustrating the different approaches. And it suggests checklists that may be used to assess research. The second part follows through the process of doing a piece of research. It suggests research questions and examples relevant to education; social stratification; health, welfare and

poverty; crime, deviance and 'social problems'. The third part may not be so relevant: how to pass a sociology course!

Everitt, A., Hardiker, P., Mullender, A. and Littlewood, J. (1992) ***Applied Research for Better Practice*, Basingstoke, Macmillan.**
Written primarily for social workers although more broadly relevant to health and social welfare practitioners, this book focuses on the practitioner-researcher, being research-minded in day-to-day practice. It starts by examining the relationship between research and practice, then looks at key ways of theorising ways of knowing, and then considers research purposes and values. The second part of the book develops a methodology for the research-minded practitioner taking account of values, ethics, purposes, communication, roles and skills. It then applies this methodology to stages of the practice process: formulating issues, preparing, groundwork and access; engaging with subjects to generate data; analysing data; evaluating practice.

Gilbert, N. (ed.) (1993) *Researching Social Life*, London, Sage.
This collection of chapters following through the process of doing research has been written by a sociology undergraduate course team. As the writers themselves say, it is, like researching, a mixture of philosophy and theory of knowledge on the one hand and practical down-to earth illustrative practical examples on the other. It covers the entire research process and is a good book to go to to find out more about particular aspects of research. It covers: discussion about the nature and purpose of social research; sampling; interview schedules, questionnaire design; attitude measurement; ethnography; documentary sources of data and secondary statistics; management and coding of data and computer analyses of survey data; conversation analysis; writing research reports.

Herbert, M. (1990) *Planning a Research Project: A Guide for Practitioners and Trainees in the Helping Professions*, London, Cassell.
Similar text to Judith Bell's. If hers was described as sociological, Martin Herbert's is psychological – more, although not solely, experimental, quantitative and statistical. It also follows through the research process: in planning your research project, ident-

ifying problems, deciding on strategy, considering quantitative or qualitative methods, assembling evidence and generating data; in doing your research, collecting and analysing data, statistical analysis and writing-up. There are useful appendices on preparing a research proposal, an illustrative example of a research proposal, a statement of ethics, a guide to reviewing research, and a guide to doing a library search.

Hopkins, D. (1985) *A Teacher's Guide to Classroom Research*, Milton Keynes, Open University Press.
This focuses on the teacher-researcher and starts by making the case for teachers to be also researchers. It is very readable and relevant for doing research in a participative way with groups other than in classrooms. It covers action-research, problem formation, data gathering, observation and analysis, and feeding the research into change processes. It has a useful appendix on ethics.

Howard, K. and Sharp, J.A. (1983) *The Management of a Student Research Project*, Aldershot, Gower.
This again follows through the research process although it is addressed primarily to university students doing a project or dissertation for their course. It covers: the situation of the research student, selecting and justifying the research topic, planning the research, searching the literature, gathering and analysing the data, common problems in doing research, presenting findings.

Sapsford, R. and Abbott, P. (1992) *Research Methods for Nurses and the Caring Professions*, Buckingham, Open University Press.
Another book for practitioners taking a slightly different focus. Very like the guide for sociology students (Dunsmuir and Williams, 1991), the first part focuses on how to assess the research done by others, the second part focuses on doing research. The first part presents summaries of pieces of research that have adopted different research approaches and suggests factors that should be borne in mind when making sense of the research, how it was done and the findings. It covers: research undertaken through open-ended interviewing; observation research; quasi-experimental research using controlled trials;

survey research; and research based on secondary (documentary) sources. The second part of the book pursues the methods of these different research approaches. The conclusion focuses on writing up and other ways of presenting research and explores the relationships between research and theory, and research and practice.

Veal, A.J. (1992) *Research Methods for Leisure and Tourism: A Practical Guide*, Harlow, Longman/ILAM.
Again, as the title implies, another book making research methods accessible to a particular occupational group. And like similar books, it follows the familiar format: why research; different research approaches; research plans and proposals; alternative research methods; searching the literature; gathering data from documentary sources; observation; qualitative methods; questionnaire surveys and design; sampling, survey analysis; writing the research report. The book is particularly useful if you are wanting to use structured methods, such as questionnaires, producing data that may be treated as quantitative and analysed statistically using computer programmes specially designed for survey analysis. It also very usefully provides guidance on setting out the final research report.

Whitaker, D.S. and Archer, J.L. (1989) *Research by Social Workers: Capitalizing on Experience*, Central Council for Education and Training in Social Work Study 9, London, CCETSW.
This manual derives from training in research methods that the two authors have provided for practising social workers. It combines research with practice and focuses on small-scale research. It starts by considering the possible purposes of research and types of research that may be undertaken by practitioners. It then follows through the research process: planning the research; designing the research; data collection; undertaking the research; analysing and presenting data; thinking about implications for policy and practice; the costs and benefits of doing research as a practitioner; structures and schemes that may be developed in organisations to enhance them in their research.

EVALUATION METHODS TEXTS

Ball, M. (1988) *Evaluation in the Voluntary Sector*, The Forbes Trust in association with CEI.
This very accessible and well-presented book on evaluation, produced in the late 1980s, arose out of a piece of research to find out what voluntary sector projects were doing about research: the problems experienced; the advice and material needed. It covers: consideration of the different 'stakeholders' in evaluation – grant-makers, voluntary organisations, consumers, researchers; the evaluation process; using an external evaluator, doing it yourself and collective approaches.

Connor, A. (1993) *Monitoring and Evaluation Made Easy: A Handbook for Voluntary Organisations*, Edinburgh, HMSO.
This handbook was been written following research undertaken into monitoring and evaluation in the voluntary sector. The research focused particularly on testing out a self-evaluation model designed to bridge the gap between evaluation and the improvement of standards. It is written for voluntary organisations wanting to evaluate themselves. It is accessible, well-presented and is particularly useful for voluntary projects engaged in the delivery of community care services.

Feuerstein, M.-T. (1986) *Partners in Evaluation: Evaluating Development and Community Programmes with Participants*, London and Basingstoke, Macmillan Education.
This is written in a very accessible style, with summary charts, check lists, exercises and cartoons. It grew out of the author's experience of working with locally-based development projects in a number of countries and is very relevant to local voluntary projects and community groups. It covers: why, for whom, when, where and how to evaluate; planning an evaluation and organising the necessary resources for it; using existing information for the evaluation; collecting additional information; reporting and presenting evaluation findings; making use of the evaluation. There is a useful glossary of terms.

van der Eyken, W. (1992) *Introducing Evaluation*, The Hague, Bernard van Leer Foundation.
This has developed from the experience of evaluation in projects around the world funded by the van Leer Foundation. It is written and illustrated in a form that is very accessible, intending that it be read by front-line practitioners rather than by researchers. It covers: planning and getting started; using information already known; keeping records; who is the evaluation for and who should do it; how to decide what to evaluate and how much will it cost; how might it be undertaken; analysing the data and presenting the findings. It includes a useful list of other materials available on research and evaluation.

The Law Centres Federation Evaluation Framework Team (1988) *Questions of Value: A Framework for the Evaluation of Law Centres*, London, Law Centres Federation.
A pack of five booklets: The Evaluation Process; The Law Centres Evaluation Profile; Evaluation Bibliography; Evaluation Case Studies; Resources for Evaluation. Obviously written for Law Centres but more generally applicable. Written and presented in a very accessible style with illustrative case studies referred to throughout. The Evaluation Process looks at: reasons to evaluate; agreeing the objectives of evaluation; the stages of evaluation; how to focus evaluation; methods for generating evaluative information; making effective use of evaluation. In addition to the references on law centres, the bibliography has two useful sections: on aspects of evaluation of advice services and related voluntary organisations; on theoretical discussion of evaluation relevant to small community organisations.

References

Abt, C.C. (ed.) (1978) *The Evaluation of Social Programs*, Beverly Hills and London, Sage.

Aldgate, J. and Tunstill, J. (1993) *National Monitoring of the Children Act; Part III, Section 17 – The First Year*, Oxford University and London, National Council for Voluntary Child Care Organisations.

Alkin, M. (1990) *Debates in Evaluation*, Newbury Park, California and London, Sage Publications.

Anyshire County Council, Social Services Department (1993) *Practice Guidance: Including Eligibility Criteria/Priorities for the Provision of Services*, Anyshire, January.

Audit Commission (1991) *The Citizen's Charter, Local Authority Performance Indicators*, London.

Bailey, J. (1980) *Ideas and Intervention: Social Theory for Practice*, London, Routledge.

Barnes, M. and Miller, N. (eds) (1988) 'Performance Measurement in Personal Social Services', *Research, Policy and Planning*, 6, (2), Special Issue, Social Services Research Group.

Barnes, M. and Wistow, G. (1994) 'Involving Carers in Planning and Review', in A. Connor and S. Black (eds), *Performance Review and Quality in Social Care*, London, Jessica Kingsley.

Barrett, M. (1991) *The Politics of Truth: From Marx to Foucault*, Cambridge, Polity Press.

Bauman, Z. (1989) *Modernity and the Holocaust*, Cambridge, Polity.

Beresford, P. and Croft, S. (1993) *Citizen Involvement: A Practical Guide for Change*, Basingstoke, Macmillan.

Biehal, N., Fisher, M., Marsh, P. and Sainsbury, E. (1992) 'Rights and Social Work', in A. Coote (ed.), *The Welfare of Citizens: Developing New Social Rights*, London, Institute for Public Policy Research/Rivers Oram Press.

Booth, T. (1988) *Developing Policy Research*, Aldershot, Avebury.

Brannen, J. (ed.) (1992) *Mixing Methods: Qualitative and Quantitative Research*, Aldershot, Avebury.

Buist, M. (1984) 'Illuminative Evaluation', in J. Lishman (ed.), *Evaluation,* Research Highlights 8, Aberdeen, Department of Social Work, University of Aberdeen.

Bulmer, M. (1982) *The Uses of Social Research: Social Investigation in Public Policy-Making,* London, Allen & Unwin.

Bulmer, M. (1986) *Social Science and Social Policy,* London, Allen & Unwin.

Burgess, R.G. (1984) *In the Field: An Introduction to Field Research,* London, Allen & Unwin.

Butler, J. (1994) 'Origins and Early Developments', in R. Robinson and J. le Grand (eds), *Evaluating the NHS Reforms,* Hermitage, Newbury, Policy Journals; London, King's Fund Institute.

Carter, N. (1988a) 'Measuring Government Performance', *Political Quarterly,* 59, (3), 369–75.

Carter, N. (1988b) 'Performance Indicators in the Criminal Justice System', in A. Harrison and J. Gretton (eds), *Crime UK 1988: An Economic and Policy Audit,* Hermitage, Newbury, Policy Journals, 87–91.

Carter, N. (1989) 'Performance Indicators: 'Back-Seat Driving' Or 'Hands-Off' Control?', *Policy & Politics,* 17, (2), 131–8.

Carter, N. (1991) 'Learning to Measure Performance: The Use of Indicators in Organisations', *Public Administration,* 69, (Spring), 85–101.

Carter, N., Klein, R. and Day, P. (1991) *How Organisations Manage Success,* London, Routledge.

Carter, P., Chan, C., Everitt, A., Ng, I. and Tsang, N.M. (1992) *Reflecting on Supervision: Supervising Students in Practice,* Hong Kong, Hong Kong Polytechnic.

Cheetham, J., Fuller, R., McIvor, G. and Petch, A. (1992) *Evaluating Social Work Effectiveness,* Buckingham, Open University Press.

Cohen, A. (1989) 'Performance Indicators: Services for Children', *Research, Policy and Planning,* 7, (2), Social Services Research Group.

Community Care (1989) *The White Paper: Birth of a Notion, Special Supplement,* 30 November, i–xii.

Compton, B.R. and Galaway, B. (1989) *Social Work Processes,* 4th edn, Belmont, Wadsworth Publishing Company.

Connor, A. and Black, S. (eds) (1994) *Performance Review and Quality in Social Care,* Research Highlights in Social Work, 20, London, Jessica Kingsley.

Connor, S. (1993) 'The Necessity of Value', in J. Squires (ed.), *Principled Positions: Postmodernism and the Rediscovery of Value,* London, Lawrence & Wishart.

Coote, A. (ed.) (1992) *The Welfare of Citizens: Developing New Social Rights,* London, Institute for Public Policy Research/ Rivers Oram Press.

Coote, A. (1994) 'Performance and Quality in Public Services', in A. Connor and S. Black (eds), *Performance Review and Quality in Social Care,* Research Highlights in Social Work, 20, London, Jessica Kingsley.

Craft, A. and the Association of Residential Care (ARC) and the National Association for Protection from Sexual Abuse of Adults and Children with Learning Disabilities (1993) *It Could Never Happen Here! The Prevention and Treatment of Sexual Abuse of Adults with Learning Disabilities in Residential Settings.*

Crompton, T. and McMillan, C. (1994) 'Going Places', *Community Care,* 10 March 1994, 28–9.

Cronbach, L. J. and Associates (1980) *Toward Reform of Program Evaluation,* San Francisco, Jossey-Bass.

Davies, B. and Challis, D. (1986) *Matching Resources to Needs in Community-Based Care,* Aldershot, Gower.

Davies, B., Bebbington, A., and Charnley, H. (1990) *Resources, Needs and Outcomes in Community-Based Care,* Aldershot, Gower.

Department of Health (1989a) *Caring for People: Community Care in the Next Decade and Beyond,* cmnd. 849, London, HMSO.

Department of Health (1989b) *The Care of Children: Principles and Practice in Regulations and Guidance,* London, HMSO.

Department of Health (1991a) *Patterns and Outcomes in Child Placement: Messages from Current Research and Their Implications,* London, HMSO.

Department of Health (1991b) *Inspecting for Quality: Guidance on Practice for Inspection Units in Social Services Departments and other Agencies,* London, Social Services Inspectorate, HMSO.

Department of Health, Social Services Inspectorate (1992) *Capitalising on the Act: A Working Party Report on the Implementation of the Children Act 1989 in London,* London.

Department of Health, Social Services Inspectorate (1993) *Inspection of Assessment and Care Management Arrangements in Social Services Departments,* London, London East Inspection Group, December.

Department of Health (1993) *Children Act Report*, London, HMSO.
Department of Health (1994) *Key Indicators of Local Authority Social Services 1991–1992*, London, Government Statistical Service.
Doyal, L. and Gough, I. (1991) *A Theory of Human Need*, Basingstoke, Macmillan.
Everitt, A. (1994) *Creating Conversations: An Evaluation of the Gateshead Elderly Arts Project*, Newcastle upon Tyne, Social Welfare Research Unit, University of Northumbria at Newcastle and Equal Arts.
Everitt, A. and Gibson, A. (1994) *Making It Work: Researching in the Voluntary Sector*, Wivenhoe, Essex, Association for Research in the Voluntary and Community Sector.
Everitt, A. and Green, J. (1995) *A Local Community Education Project: An Evaluation*, Social Welfare Research Unit, University of Northumbria at Newcastle.
Everitt, A., Hardiker, P., Littlewood, J. and Mullender, A. (1992) *Applied Research for Better Practice*, London, Macmillan.
Everitt, A. and Johnson, C. (1992) *A Young Women's Project: An Evaluation*, Social Welfare Research Unit, University of Northumbria at Newcastle.
Fay, B. (1975) *Social Theory and Political Practice*, London, George Allen & Unwin.
Fay, B. (1987) *Critical Social Science: Liberation and its Limits*, Oxford, Blackwell and Polity Press.
Finch, J. (1989) *Family Obligations and Social Change*, Cambridge and Oxford, Polity Press in association with Basil Blackwell.
Fischer, J. (1976) *The Effectiveness of Social Casework*, Springfield, Illinois, Charles C. Thomas.
Flynn, N. (1989) 'The "New Right" and Social Policy', *Policy & Politics*, 17, (2), 97–110.
Foucault, M. (1968) 'Politics and the Study of Discourse' (translated from an article in *Esprit*), *Ideology and Consciousness*, (1978) 3, 7–26.
Foucault, M. (1979) *Discipline and Punish: The Birth of the Prison*, New York, Vintage.
Fox, N. J. (1993) *Post-Modernism, Sociology and Health*, Buckingham, Open University Press.
Fraser, N. (1989) 'Talking About Needs: Interpretative Contests as Political Conflicts in Welfare State Societies', *Ethics*, 99, (January), 291–313.

Freire, P. (1972) *Pedagogy of the Oppressed,* Harmondsworth, Penguin.

Friend, B. and Ivory, M. (1994) 'Fragmentation Leads to Chaos', *Community Care,* 17 March 1994, 3.

Gardner, R. (1992) *Preventing Family Breakdown,* London, National Children's Bureau.

George, V. and Miller, S. (eds) (1994) *Social Policy Towards 2000: Squaring the Welfare Circle,* London, Routledge.

Glyn, A. and Miliband, D. (1994) *Paying for Inequality: The Economic Costs of Social Injustice,* London, IPPR/Rivers Oram Press.

Gold, N. (1981) *The Stakeholder Process in Educational Program Evaluation,* Washington DC, National Institute of Education.

Goldberg, E.M. and Connelly, N. (eds) (1981) *Evaluative Research in Social Care,* London, Heinemann Educational Books.

Goodin, R.E. (1985) *Protecting the Vulnerable: A Reanalysis of Our Social Responsibilities,* London, University of Chicago Press.

Goold, M. and Campbell, A. (1987) *Strategies and Styles,* Oxford, Blackwell.

Gordon, K.H. (1991) 'Improving Practice Through Illuminative Evaluation', *Social Services Review,* 65, (3), 365–78.

Gray, A. and Jenkins, B. (1993) 'Markets, Managers and the Public Service: The Changing of a Culture', in P. Taylor-Gooby and R. Lawson (eds), *Markets and Managers: New Issues in the Delivery of Welfare,* Buckingham, Open University Press.

Gray, A.G. and Jenkins, W.I. with Flynn, A.C. and Rutherford, B.A. (1991) 'The Management of Change in Whitehall: The Experience of the FMI', *Public Administration,* 69 (1), 41–59.

Green, J. (1992) 'The Community Development Project Revisited', in P. Carter, T. Jeffs and M.K. Smith (eds), *Changing Social Work and Welfare,* Buckingham, Open University Press.

Green, J. (1994) *Talking with Children, Report to the City Challenge Board,* Newcastle upon Tyne, Social Welfare Research Unit, University of Northumbria at Newcastle.

Griffiths, R. (1988) *Community Care: Agenda for Action,* London, HMSO.

Guba, E.G. and Lincoln, Y.S. (1981) *Effective Evaluation,* San Francisco, Jossey-Bass.

Guba, E.G. and Lincoln, Y.S. (1989) *Fourth Generation Evaluation,* Newbury Park, California and London, Sage Publications.

Gunn, L. (1978) 'Why Is Implementation So Difficult?', *Management Services in Government*, November.

Hadley, R. and Hatch, S. (1981) *Social Welfare and the Failure of the State*, London, Allen & Unwin.

Hallett, C. (1991) 'The Children Act 1989 and Community Care: Comparisons and Contrasts', *Policy & Politics*, 19, (4), 283–291.

Halsey, A. H. (1974) 'Government Against Poverty in School and Community', in M. Bulmer (ed.), *Social Policy Research*, London, Allen & Unwin.

Hardiker, P. (1979) 'The Role of Probation Officers in Sentencing', in H. Parker (ed.), *Social Work and the Courts*, London, Arnold.

Hardiker, P. (1992a) 'Family Support Services and Children with Disabilities', in J. Gibbons (ed.), *The Children Act 1989 and Family Support: Principles into Practice*, London, HMSO.

Hardiker, P. (1992b) *Impetus for Change in Anyshire Social Services Department: A Preliminary Evaluation*, University of Leicester, School of Social Work, Research Report.

Hardiker, P. (1993) *Research in Social Work: Process, Promises and Payoffs*, Paper delivered at a Social Work Research Conference, The Queen's University, Belfast, May.

Hardiker, P. (1994a) 'Thinking and Practising Otherwise: Disability and Child Abuse', *Disability and Society*, Review Article, 9, (2), 257–64.

Hardiker, P. (1994b) 'The Social Policy Contexts of Services to Prevent Unstable Family Life', in J. Lewis (ed.), *Family and Parenthood Seminar Papers*, York, Joseph Rowntree Foundation.

Hardiker, P. (1994c) 'Windows on the Worlds of Life, Work and Welfare: Joy and Pain, Liberation and Oppression', *Disability and Society*, 9 (3), 237–41.

Hardiker, P. and Barker, M. (eds) (1981) *Theories of Practice in Social Work*, London, Academic Press.

Hardiker, P. and Barker, M. (1991) 'Towards Social Theory for Social Work', in J. Lishman (ed.) *Handbook of Theory for Practice Teachers in Social Work*, London, Jessica Kingsley.

Hardiker, P. and Barker, M. (1994a) *The 1989 Children Act: Social Work Processes, Social Policy Contexts and 'Significant Harm'*, University of Leicester, School of Social Work, Research Report.

Hardiker, P. and Barker, M. (1994b) *Implementing the NHS and Community Care Act, 1990: Needs-Led Assessment and Care Packages,* Leicester, University of Leicester, School of Social Work, Research Project.

Hardiker, P., Exton, K. and Barker, M. (1991a) 'Analysing Policy–Practice Links in Preventive Childcare', in P. Carter, T. Jeffs and M.K. Smith (eds), *Social Work and Social Welfare Yearbook 3,* Milton Keynes, Open University Press.

Hardiker, P., Exton, K. and Barker, M. (1991b) *Policies and Practices in Preventive Child Care,* Avebury, Gower.

Hardiker, P., Exton, K. and Barker, M. (1991c) 'The Social Policy Contexts of Prevention in Child Care', *British Journal of Social Work,* 21 (4), 341–59.

Hardiker, P., Pedley, J., Littlewood, J. and Olley, D. (1986) 'Coping with Chronic Renal Failure', *British Journal of Social Work,* 16 (2), 203–22.

Hawtin, M., Hughes, G. and Percy-Smith, J. (1994) *Community Profiling: Auditing Social Needs,* Buckingham, Open University Press.

Heath, A., Colton, M. and Aldgate, J. (1989) 'Educational Progress of Children In and Out of Care', *British Journal of Social Work,* 19 (6), 447–60.

Hills, J., Glennister, H. and Le Grand, J. (1993) *Investigating Welfare: Final Report of the ESRC Welfare Research Programme,* London, London School of Economics, Sutory-Toyota International Centre.

Hoggett, B. (1989) 'The Children Bill: The Aim', *Family Law,* 19, 217–19.

Hoggett, P. and Hambleton, R. (eds) (1987) *Decentralisation and Democracy,* Occasional Paper No. 28, School for Advanced Urban Studies, University of Bristol.

Holland, J. and Ramazanoglu, C. (1994) 'Coming to Conclusions: Power and Interpretation in Researching Young Women's Sexuality', in M. Maynard and J. Purvis (eds), *Researching Women's Lives from a Feminist Perspective,* London, Taylor & Francis.

Hooper, C.A. (1992) 'Child Sexual Abuse and the Regulation of Women: Variations on a Theme', in C. Smart (ed.), *Regulating Womanhood: Historical Essays on Marriage, Motherhood and Sexuality,* London, Routledge.

Hopkins, J. (1990) 'A Competence Based Approach to the Care of Children', *Adoption and Fostering,* 14 (4), 18–22.

House, E.R. (ed.) (1986) *New Directions in Educational Evaluation*, London, Falmer.

House, E.R. (1993) *Professional Evaluation: Social Impact and Political Consequences*, Newbury Park, California and London, Sage Publications.

Howe, D. (1994) 'Modernity, Postmodernity and Social Work', *British Journal of Social Work*, 24, 513–32.

Hoyes, L., Means, R. and Le Grand, J. (1992) *Made to Measure? Performance Indicators, Performance Measurement and the Reform of Community Care*, Bristol, School for Advanced Urban Studies.

Hudson, A. (1989) '"Troublesome Girls": Towards Alternative Definitions and Policies', in M.Cain (ed.), *Growing Up Good: Policing the Behaviour of Girls in Europe*, London, Sage.

In Need Implementation Group (1991) *The Children Act and Children's Needs: Make It The Answer Not The Problem*, London, NCVCCVO.

Jackson, P. (1988a) 'The Management of Performance in the Public Sector', *Public Money & Management*, Winter, 11–16.

Jackson, P.M. (1988b) *Measuring the Efficiency of the Public Sector*, Manchester Statistical Society, Paper presented on 13 December.

Jackson, P.M. and Palmer, M. (1992) *Developing Performance Monitoring in Public Sector Organisations*, Leicester, University of Leicester, Management Centre.

Jeffs, T. and Smith, M. (eds) (1990) *Using Informal Education: An alternative to casework, teaching and control?*, Milton Keynes, Open University Press.

Jones, A. (1991) *Report of the Black Communities Care Project*, Leeds, National Institute for Social Work.

Jones, Stedman, E. (1971) *Outcast London*, Oxford, Clarendon Press.

Judge, K. and Solomon, M. (1993) 'Public Opinion and the National Health Service: Patterns and Perspectives in Consumer Satisfaction', *Journal of Social Policy*, 22, (3), 299–327.

Kelly, L., Burton, S., and Regan, L. (1994) 'Researching Women's Lives or Studying Women's Oppression? Reflections on What Constitutes Feminist Research', in M. Maynard and J. Purvis (eds), *Researching Women's Lives from a Feminist Perspective*, London, Taylor & Francis.

Kirkwood, A. (1993) *The Leicestershire Inquiry: The Report of an Inquiry into Aspects of the Management of Children's Homes in*

Leicestershire Between 1973 and 1986, Leicestershire County Council.

Knapp, M. (1989) *Measuring Child Care Outcomes*, University of Kent at Canterbury; Personal Social Services Research Unit: Discussion Paper 630.

Layder, D. (1993) *New Strategies in Social Research*, Cambridge, Polity Press.

Levy, A. and Kahan, B. (1991) *The Pindown Experience and the Protection of Children: The Report of the Staffordshire Child Care Inquiry, 1990*, Staffordshire County Council.

Lipsky, M. (1980) *Street Level Bureaucracy*, New York, Russell Sage.

Lishman, J. (ed.) (1991) *Evaluation*, Research Highlights in Social Work, 8, 2nd edn, London, Jessica Kingsley.

Lukes, S. (1974) *Power: A Radical View*, London and Basingstoke, Macmillan.

Marris, P. and Rein, M. (1967) *Dilemmas of Social Reform: Poverty and Community Action in the United States*, London, Routledge & Kegan Paul.

Masson, J. (1990) *The Children Act 1989: Text and Commentary*, London, Sweet & Maxwell.

Maynard, M. (1994) 'Methods, Practice and Epistemology: The Debate about Feminism and Research', in M. Maynard and J. Purvis (eds), *Researching Women's Lives from a Feminist Perspective*, London, Taylor & Francis.

Maynard, M. and Purvis, J. (eds) (1994) *Researching Women's Lives from a Feminist Perspective*, London, Taylor & Francis.

Mayo, M. (1994) *Communities and Caring: The Mixed Economy of Welfare*, Basingstoke, Macmillan.

Mills, C.W. (1959) *The Sociological Imagination*, London, Oxford University Press.

Morris, J. (1993) 'Key Task I: Assessment', in *Community Care: Implementing the Community Care Act: The 8 Key Tasks*, Sutton, Reed Business Publishing, 2.

National Community Development Project (1973) *Inter-Project Report*, London, CDP Information and Intelligence Unit.

National Institute for Social Work (1988) *Residential Care: A Positive Choice – Report of the Independent Review of Residential Care*, Wagner Report, London, NISW/HMSO.

Nicolaus, M. (1973) 'The Professional Organization of Sociology: A View from Below', in R. Blackburn (ed.) *Ideology in*

Social Science: Readings in Critical Social Theory, London, Fontana/Collins.

NOW Joint Evaluation and Development Project (1995) *Training European Women: new opportunities for women in four European cities*, Social Welfare Research Unit, University of Northumbria at Newcastle.

Oakley A. (1990) 'Who's Afraid of the Randomized Controlled Trial? Some Dilemmas of the Scientific Method and "Good" Research Practice', in H. Roberts (ed.), *Women's Health Counts*, London and New York, Routledge.

O'Brien, J. (1989) 'A Guide to Personal Futures Planning', in G.T. Bellamy and B. Wilcox (eds), *A Comprehensive Guide to the Activities Catalogue: An Alternative Curriculum for Youth and Adults with Severe Disabilities*, Baltimore, Maryland, Paul H. Brookes.

Oliver, M. (1992) 'Changing the Social Relations of Research Production?', *Disability, Handicap and Society*, Special Issue: Researching Disability, 7, (2), 101–14.

Ozolins, R. and Tunstill, J. (1994) *Voluntary Child Care Organisations after the 1989 Children Act*, London, National Council for Voluntary Child Care Organisations.

Parker, R. (1988) 'An Historical Background', in I. Sinclair (ed.), *Residential Care: The Research Reviewed*, London, HMSO, National Institute for Social Work.

Parker, R., Ward, H., Jackson, S., Aldgate, J. and Wedge, P. (eds) (1992) *Looking After Children: Assessing Outcomes in Child Care*, London, HMSO.

Parlett, M. and Hamilton, D. (1976) 'Evaluation as Illumination: A New Approach to the Study of Innovatory Programs', in G.V. Glass (ed.), *Evaluation Studies Review Annual 1979*, California, Sage.

Parry, R. (ed.) (1990) *Privatisation*, London, Jessica Kingsley.

Parton, N. (1994a) ' The Nature of Social Work Under Conditions of (Post) Modernity', *Social Work & Social Sciences Review*, 5, (2), 93–112.

Parton, N. (1994b) '"Problematics of Government", (Post) Modernity and Social Work', *British Journal of Social Work*, 24, 9–32.

Payne, M. (1991) *Modern Social Work Theory: A Critical Introduction*, Basingstoke, Macmillan.

Phillips, C., Palfrey, C. and Thomas, P. (1994) *Evaluating Health and Social Care*, Basingstoke and London, Macmillan.

Plant, R., Lesser, H. and Taylor-Gooby, P. (1980) *Political Philosophy and Social Welfare: Essays on the Normative Basis of Welfare Provision*, London, Routledge.

Pollitt, C. (1988) 'Bringing Consumers into Performance Measurement', *Policy & Politics*, 16, (2), 77–87.

Pollitt, C. (1990) *Managerialism and the Public Services*, Oxford, Blackwell.

Rees, S. and Wallace, A. (1982) *Verdicts on Social Work*, London, Edward Arnold.

Rein, M. (1976) *Social Science and Public Policy*, Harmondsworth, Penguin.

Reith, D. (1984) 'Evaluation: A Function of Practice', in J. Lishman (ed.), *Evaluation*, Research Highlights 8, Aberdeen, Department of Social Work, University of Aberdeen.

Richmond, M.E. (1917) *Social Diagnosis*, New York, Russell Sage Foundation.

Robbins, D. (ed.) (1993) *Community Care: Findings from Department of Health Funded Research 1988–1992*, London, HMSO.

Robinson, R. and Le Grand, J. (eds) (1994) *Evaluating the NHS Reforms*, Hermitage, Newbury, Policy Journals, King's Fund Institute.

Rojek, C., Peacock, G. and Collins, S. (1988) *Social Work and Received Ideas*, London, Routledge.

Royal College of Nursing (1994) *Nursing and Child Protection*, London.

Russell, B. (1974) *History of Western Philosophy and its Connection with Political and Social Circumstances from the Earliest Times to the Present Day*, London, Allen & Unwin.

Ryan, W. (1971) *Blaming the Victim*, London, Orbach & Chambers.

Sainsbury, E. (1987) 'Client Studies: Their Contribution and Limitations in Influencing Social Work Practice', *British Journal of Social Work*, 17 (6), 635–44.

Schick, A. (1990) 'Budgeting for Results: Adaptation to Fiscal Stress in Industrial Democracies', *Public Administration Review*, 50, (1), 26–34.

Shaw, M., Masson, J. and Brocklesby, E. (1991) *Children in Need and Their Families: A New Approach, A Manual for Managers on Part II of the Children Act, 1989*, Leicester, University of Leicester,

School of Social Work and Faculty of Law, and Department of Health.

Sinclair, I. (ed) (1990) *Kaleidoscope of Care: Review of Research on Welfare Provision for Elderly People*, London, National Institute for Social Work.

Smith, G. and Cantley, C. (1985) *Assessing Health Care: A Study in Organisational Evaluation*, Milton Keynes, Open University Press.

Smyth, J. (1991) *Teachers as Collaborative Learners: Challenging Dominant Forms of Supervision*, Milton Keynes, Open University Press.

Squires, J. (ed.) (1993) *Principled Positions: Postmodernism and the Rediscovery of Value*, London, Lawrence & Wishart.

Stake, R.E. and Denny, T. (1969) 'Needed Concepts and Techniques for Utilizing More Fully the Potential of Evaluation', *National Society for the Study of Education Yearbook, LXV111, Part 11*, Chicago, University of Chicago Press.

Streather, J. (1989) *Prevention of Family Breakdown*, Paper presented at Conference at the National Children's Bureau, London, 8 November (unpublished).

Taylor-Gooby, P. and Lawson, R. (1993) *Markets and Managers: New Issues in the Delivery of Welfare*, Buckingham, Open University Press.

Thomson, W. (1992) 'Realising Rights through Local Service Contracts', in A. Coote (ed.), *The Welfare of Citizens: Developing New Social Rights*, London, Institute for Public Policy Research/Rivers Oram Press.

Townsend, P. (1981) 'Guerrillas, Subordinates and Passers-By: The Relationship Between Sociologists and Social Policy', *Critical Social Policy*, 1, (2), 22–34.

Tunstill, J. (1994) 'What Services Currently Address the Onset of Problems', in J. Lewis (ed.), *Joseph Rowntree Foundation, Family and Parenthood Seminar Papers*, Paper 8, York.

Walby, S. (1990) *Theorizing Patriarchy*, Oxford, Basil Blackwell.

Walker, A. (1989) 'Community Care', in M. McCarthy (ed.), *The New Politics of Welfare: An Agenda for the 1990s*, London, Macmillan.

Wardhaugh, J. and Wilding, P. (1993) 'Towards an Explanation of the Corruption of Care', *Critical Social Policy*, 13, (1), 4–31.

Ware, A. and Goodin, R.E. (eds) (1990) *Needs and Welfare*, London, Sage.

Warner, N. (1994) *Community Care: Just A Fairy Tale*, London, Carers National Association.

Weedon, C. (1987) *Feminist Practice & Post-structuralist Theory*, Oxford, Blackwell.

Weiss, C.H. (ed.) (1977) *Using Social Research in Policy Making*, Lexington, Mass., D.C. Heath.

Weiss, C.H. (1986a) 'Research and Policy-Making: A Limited Partnership', in F. Heller (ed.), *The Use and Abuse of Social Science*, London, Sage.

Weiss, C.H. (1986b) 'The Stakeholder Approach to Evaluation: Origins and Promise', in E. House (ed.), *New Directions in Educational Evaluation*, London, Falmer.

Whan, M. (1986) 'On the Nature of Practice', *British Journal of Social Work*, 16, 243–50.

Whitaker, D. Stock (1992) 'Making Research a Part of Group Therapeutic Practice', *Group Analysis*, 25, 433–48.

Whitaker, D. Stock and Archer, J.L. (1989) *Research by Social Workers: Capitalising on Experience*, Study 9, London, CCETSW.

Whitmore, E. (1991) 'Evaluation and Empowerment: It's Process That Counts', *Empowerment and Family Support*, 2, (2), September, New York, Cornell Empowerment Project.

Whittaker, A. (1994) 'Service Evaluation By People With Learning Difficulties', in A. Connor and S. Black (eds), *Performance Review and Quality in Social Care*, London, Jessica Kingsley.

Willis, A. (1991) *Probation Orders with Requirements: A Consumer Survey*, (5 vols), Leicester, University of Leicester, School of Social Work.

Author Index

Abt, C.C. 42
Aldgate, J. & Tunstill, J. 119, 120
Alkin, M. 133, 150
Anyshire Social Services Department 124, 125

Barnes, M. & Miller, M. 57
Barnes, M. & Wistow, C. 127
Barrett, M. 105
Beresford, P. & Croft, S. 142
Biehal, N. *et al.* 177, 178
Booth, T. 44
Brannen, J. 138, 194
Buist, M. 88
Bulmer, M. 43, 44
Burgess, R.G. 129

Carter, N. 62, 63, 64, 65, 69, 70, 71
Carter, P. *et al.* 155
Cheetham, J. *et al.* 48
Cohen, A. 58, 59
Connor, A. 169, 170, 174
Coote, A. 140, 141
Craft, A. 31
Cronbach, L.J. *et al.* 44

Department of Health 119, 120, 124, 139
Doyal, L. & Gough, I. 185

Everitt, A. 28, 38, 91, 180
Everitt, A. & Gibson, A. 23, 146, 167, 168
Everitt, A. & Green, J. 22
Everitt, A., Hardiker, P., Mullender, A. and Littlewood, J. 21, 23, 29, 172
Everitt, A. & Johnson, C. 101

Fay, B. 187, 188
Finch, J. 184
Foucault, M. 106, 112, 173
Fox, N.J. 108, 117, 144, 149, 151, 161, 175, 176, 179, 183
Fraser, N. 108, 112, 113, 114, 115, 117, 127, 134, 135, 161, 175, 176, 179, 183
Freire, P. 151, 178

Gold, N. 86
Goodin, R.E. 184, 185
Goold, M. & Campbell, A. 73
Gordon, K.H. 88, 89
Gray, A. & Jenkins, B. 145
Green, J. 43, 147
Guba, E.G. & Lincoln, Y.S. 86, 91, 95, 96, 97, 135, 166, 167, 178
Gunn, L. 74

Hallett, C. 123
Halsey, A.M. 43
Hardiker, P. 81, 120, 128, 150, 189
Hardiker, P. & Barker, M. 60, 121, 136, 189, 190
Hardiker, P., Exton, K. & Barker, M. 66, 67, 118, 122, 189
Hills, J. *et al.* 185
Holland, J. & Ramazanoglu, C. 165, 168, 169
Hooper, C.A. 173
House, E.R. 19, 27, 50, 133, 135, 150, 167
Hoyes, L. *et al.* 67, 68, 73
Howe, D. 179, 180
Hudson, A. 173

In Need Implementation Group 119, 121

Jackson, P. 58, 73
Jones, A. 71

Judge, K. & Solomon, M. 143, 144, 145

Kelly, L., Burton, S. & Regan, L. 157
Kirkwood, A. 31
Knapp, M. 60, 61

Layder, D. 108, 109, 110, 111, 112, 127, 131, 183
Levy, A. & Kahan, B. 31
Lipsky, M. 44, 64
Lukes, S. 97

Marris, P. & Rein, M. 43
Masson, J. 119
Maynard, M. 163, 168
Mayo, M. 190
Mills, C.W. 29, 131

National Community Development Project 43
National Institute for Social Work 123
NAYPIC 38
Nicolaus, M. 29
NOW Joint Evaluation and Development Programme 154

Oakley, A. 51
Oliver, M. 158
Ozolins, R. & Tunstill, J. 121

Parlett, M. & Hamilton, D. 86, 88
Parton, N. 41, 42, 173, 174
Payne, M. *et al.* 183
Phillips, C., Palfrey, C. & Thomas, P. 47, 48
Plant, R. *et al.* 183
Pollitt, C. 47, 71

Rees, S. & Wallace, A. 86, 143
Rein, M. 42
Reith, D. 88
Richmond, Mary 190
Robbins, D. 123
Rojek, C., Peacock, G. & Collins, S. 173
Russell, Bertrand 172
Ryan, W. 195

Sainsbury, E. 138
Shaw, M. *et al.* 119
Sinclair, I. *et al.* 123
Smith, G. & Cantley, C. 85, 86, 87, 92, 93, 94, 160
Smyth, J. 155
Stake, R.E. and Denny, T. 52
Streather, J. 119

Thomson, W. 179
Townsend, P. 119, 120
Tunstill, J. 119, 120

Walby, S. 183
Wardaugh, J. & Wilding, P. 31, 32
Ware, A. & Goodin, R.E. 185
Weedon, C. 106
Weiss, C.H. 40, 41, 42, 44, 84, 90, 92, 138
Whan, M. 171
Whitaker, D. 23, 127, 146, 152, 179
Whitaker, D. & Archer, J.L. 23
Whitmore, E. 73
Willis, A. 144

Subject Index

abuse 32–5, 37–8
accountability 1, 12, 14, 15, 19, 34, 41, 49, 57, 62–6, 141, 167–9
action-research 43, 88, 142, 158
age 10, 17, 20, 22, 24, 26, 32–5, 37–8, 38–40, 58–9, 60–2, 79, 90–1, 99, 100, 103, 104, 111, 114, 160, 161, 164, 193
analysis 23, 162–6
arts 28, 37–8, 56, 90–1, 180
assessment of needs 75, 112–31
Audit Commission 16

Beveridge 13
biography 131, 137, 149–54
British Attitudes Survey 143
British Standards Institute 140
budgetary control 41, 62–6, 125, 159
bureaucracy 14, 15, 17, 32, 33, 40, 62–6, 69, 72, 143

Cabinet Office 14
carers 12, 69, 126
causality 38, 46, 47, 48, 51–3, 55, 62, 64, 66, 72, 75, 83, 105
Community Development Projects 43
Central Policy Review Staff 14
Child Abuse Studies Unit 157
Child Poverty Action Group 116
Children Act 8, 9–11, 16, 60–2, 65, 75, 118–22, 123, 135, 139
children under five 58–9
Children's Legal Centre 116
children's services 10, 31–5, 71, 74–5, 116, 128–30, 147
CIPFA 68
citizen charters 1, 139
citizenship 1, 71–2, 162
client satisfaction 11, 76, 80, 138, 143–5, 150
clients 31–5, 71–3
commissioning evaluation 16, 25, 169
commodification 25
community 24, 27, 39, 119, 147
community care 16, 65, 75, 122–7, 128–30, 139, 154
community development 10, 22, 43, 189
community education 22, 24, 145, 152
comparative 58–9, 69, 70, 78, 81
complaints 1, 33–4, 35, 127, 140, 195
consciousness-raising 103, 152, 161
consumerism 1, 71–3, 141–3
context of practice 13–18, 25–6, 27, 29, 41, 61, 74, 89, 98, 110–12, 108–31, 135, 191
contracting 25, 75
controlled trials 39, 46, 47, 51
conversation 26, 28–9, 33, 55, 112–18, 127–8, 139, 144, 147–9, 179–81
co-option of evaluation 19, 46
corporate management 14, 76–8
corrupt practice 17, 31–5
crime statistics 65, 69–70
criminal justice 1, 8, 9–11, 15, 69–79, 82, 83, 117, 143
critical evaluation 6–13, 26, 27–36, 53–6, 67, 68, 75–6, 98–107, 112, 117, 122, 140, 148, 158, 160–2, 182, 190–6

critical theory 84, 97–9, 137, 187–8
customer care 33

data analysis 23, 162–6
data generation 23, 146–56, 162–6
debate 6, 7, 33, 34–5, 50, 53, 64, 95, 101, 102, 194
decentralisation 14, 15, 63, 64–5
decontextualisation 25–6, 85
democracy 1, 13, 15–17, 19, 75, 99, 114, 118, 142, 148, 174–81
Department of Education and Science 43
Department of Health 139–40, 154
design of evaluation 51, 108–31
devolved budgeting 17
dialogue 6, 11, 27, 32–3, 39, 54, 99, 101, 103, 134–5, 149–56, 179–81
dichotomising 32, 108, 109–12
disability 17, 20, 22, 24, 26, 28, 32, 98, 99, 100, 103, 104, 114, 116, 124, 126, 158, 159, 160, 161, 164, 179–80, 189, 193
Disability Action North East 116
discharge rates 5
disciplines 105
discourses 106, 108, 109, 112–31, 134–5, 138, 140, 142–4, 149–52, 193
discursive fields 106, 135
domestic sphere 115–16
domiciliary 12, 124

EC NOW 152–3
economic exclusion 152–3
economy, efficiency, effectiveness 1, 13–18, 19, 25, 42, 51–2, 60, 62–6, 69
education 15, 22, 25, 38–40, 43, 73, 88, 116, 145, 153–4
Educational Priority Areas 43
efficiency scrutinies 15, 62
equal opportunities 20, 72, 77–8, 129, 142
equality 17, 26, 28, 99, 100, 118, 141, 193
empowerment 6, 17, 28, 35, 71, 103, 141, 143, 194
enabling authority 16
ethnicity 10, 11, 20, 22, 77–8, 79, 100–1, 164, 193
evaluation and social control 1, 62–6
evaluation, commissioning of 16, 25, 169
evaluation, co-option of 19, 46
evaluation design 51, 108–31
evaluation for learning 37, 152
evaluation history 42–6
evaluation models
  critical 6–13, 26, 27–36, 53–6, 67, 68, 75–6, 98–107, 112, 117, 122, 140, 148, 158, 160–2, 182, 190–6
  external 5, 23, 28, 37–8, 52
  formative 86, 88
  fourth-generation 86, 95–8
  illuminative 86, 88–9
  interpretivist 86–8, 159–60
  managerial 1, 19, 26, 38–41, 42, 55, 83–5, 105, 141
  ongoing 132–4, 150
  participatory 142
  pluralist 73, 86, 92–5
  serial 132
  stakeholder 86, 89–92, 92–5, 100–1, 121, 135–6, 159–60
  summative 88
evaluation, politics of 25, 50, 94, 112–31, 135, 167
evaluation purposes 19–36, 49, 83
evaluation questions 2, 21–3, 24–5, 34, 81–3, 89, 102, 107, 134, 151–3
evaluative organisations 2, 55, 132–4, 150, 154–6
evaluator responsibilities 92, 94, 97, 139, 166–70, 178

evidence 3, 4, 8, 17, 20, 25, 47, 48, 49, 51, 53, 75, 79, 89–90, 95, 99–100, 104, 109, 134, 162–6
external evaluations 5, 23, 28, 37–8, 52

family support 120–3
family values 171
feasibility 148–9
federally funded programmes 42
feedback 24, 42, 44
feminism 100, 115–6, 152, 157–8, 163–5, 173
financial data 16, 58, 60–2
Financial Management Initiative 15, 63
formative evaluation 86, 88
fourth-generation evaluation 86, 95–8
funding 39, 45
funding of voluntary sector 22, 25, 26, 30, 37

gatekeepers 148–9
gender 10, 17, 22, 24, 26, 32, 98–100, 103, 109, 111, 114–15, 144, 157–8, 159, 160, 161, 164, 193
'good' practice 1, 6, 7, 8, 9, 17, 18, 24, 27–36, 49, 50–3, 53–6, 73, 76, 79, 81, 83–4, 90, 95, 107, 118, 135, 141, 145, 157, 162, 170–4, 176–7, 182, 188–90
grey power 116
group work 38–40, 153–4, 189

health authorities 25
health care 51, 73, 92, 144–5, 150–1, 160
historical accounts 22, 98, 110, 127, 191
history of evaluation 42–6
Home Office 43
Home Office Inspectorate of Probation 81

housing 16, 65, 124

ideology 100, 103–4, 161, 193
illuminative evaluation 86, 88–9
impact 26, 69
information technology 15, 62
inputs 10, 11, 46, 47, 53, 61, 72, 75, 79, 83, 105, 107
inspection 1, 57, 139–40
Institute of Economic Affairs 15
instrumentalism 45, 46, 51
interpretivism 7, 10, 75, 84, 86–8, 98, 105, 112–13, 137
interpretivist evaluation 86–8, 159–60
interviewing 137

judgement-making 2, 3, 4–5, 8, 17, 20, 21, 24, 48, 49, 50, 52–3, 64, 73, 76, 79, 90, 95–7, 99–100, 103–4, 107, 113, 117–18, 122, 127, 135, 141, 157–81
justice 17, 29, 99–100, 118

Keynes, J.M. 13

legitimacy 27, 32, 34, 41, 45, 53, 55, 113
local authorities 25, 28, 100, 124–5
local authority profiles 16, 76
Lord Chancellor's Department 69–70

managerial evaluation 1, 19, 26, 38–41, 42, 55, 83–5, 105, 141
managerialism 14, 26, 41, 42, 45, 71, 85, 105, 140, 143
management committees 22, 23, 26, 30, 100
management information systems 15, 45, 57
market economy 13, 19, 69, 72, 83
measurement 16, 28, 37, 40,

45, 46, 47, 51, 52, 55, 57– 82, 85
medical model 37–8, 46
mission statements 33
Model Cities Administration 138
monitoring 16, 20, 41, 73, 75, 76–9, 80, 140

NAYPIC 38
needs 16, 61, 71, 112–31, 159, 161, 173, 175–7, 183–6
neutrality 38–40, 45, 46, 47, 54, 85, 94, 105
New Public Sector Management 15, 45, 50, 62–6
New Right 16, 71
National Health Service 70, 71, 126
National Health Service and Community Care Act 1, 8, 12, 16, 122–7, 139
numerical data 12, 47, 58–9, 76–8

objectifying 32, 55, 162
objectives 23, 28, 30, 33, 57, 58, 59, 60, 62, 65, 66, 70, 74, 76–81, 85, 113, 158
objectivity 38–40, 45, 46, 47, 54, 85, 94, 105, 108
older people 28, 37–8, 90–1, 111, 123–4, 140, 146, 180, 189
ongoing evaluation 132–4, 150
openness 35, 55, 103, 195
otherness 34–5, 55, 104, 195
outcomes 11, 21, 26, 37, 46, 47, 51, 55, 61–2, 73, 75, 84, 88, 107
outputs 6, 10, 11, 16, 40, 46, 47, 53, 63, 70, 72, 73, 74, 75, 83, 84, 105
Outrage! 116

participatory evaluation 142
performance indicators 1, 7, 57–9
performance measurement 1, 7, 14, 16, 40, 45, 57–83, 126, 128–30, 137, 140
permission 148–9, 151
planning 14, 62–6
pluralist evaluation 73, 86, 92–5
policy change 11, 12, 31, 38, 43–4, 85–6, 90, 99, 115, 128–30, 193
policy goals 31, 74
policy-making and implementation 20, 21, 22, 26, 43–4, 73, 75, 115, 128–30
political economy 1, 13, 13–18, 74, 98, 115–16, 126, 131, 181–90
politics of evaluation 25, 50, 94, 112–31, 135, 107
positivism 47, 48, 49, 55, 62, 72, 75, 83, 105, 137, 143
postmodernism 7, 8, 84, 97–8, 105–7, 108–18, 122, 135, 141, 149–52, 161–2, 169–71, 173, 174–7, 183
power 6, 28, 32, 35, 53, 54, 71–5, 84, 97–8, 102–3, 105, 140, 143, 145, 149, 157–8, 160–2, 191, 194
powerlessness 32, 35, 54, 97–8, 141, 143, 145, 157, 194
practice 2, 4–6, 11, 13, 28–9, 38, 47, 70, 83, 89, 94, 109–12, 133, 134–7, 146, 148, 161–3, 171, 176–7
practice change 11–2, 38–40, 43–4, 76–9, 85–6, 90, 99, 128–30, 193
practitioners 4–6, 18, 23, 26, 28, 34, 38–40, 41, 43, 44, 46, 52, 53, 55, 65, 75–6, 83, 91, 100, 133, 134–7, 154–6, 192
prediction 47
pressure groups 116, 131
privatisation 45, 117, 119, 125, 159

probability 48, 50
probation 8, 15, 75, 76–82, 83, 142–3
process 23, 24, 25, 68–9, 86–9, 94, 96, 99, 105, 132–5
professional standards 19, 32–5, 40, 64, 81, 131, 141, 172, 173, 177
professionalism 19, 82, 143
Programme Analysis and Review 14
public expenditure plans 13, 14, 16, 17, 57, 62–6
public sector management 15, 45, 50, 62–6
purpose 23, 55, 59, 63–4, 103, 195
purposes of evaluation 19–36, 83

qualititative approaches 8, 87, 93, 99, 129, 144
quality control 1, 57–82, 85, 140
quality of life 28
quantitative approaches 8, 47, 57–82, 83, 99, 137, 144
quasi-experimental 39, 46, 51–2, 73
quasi-markets 17

race and racism 17, 26, 32, 77–8, 98–9, 100–1, 103, 104, 114, 115, 144, 159, 160, 161
randomised trials 51
rational-technical 6, 7, 8, 9–10, 27, 32, 35, 43, 50, 51, 53, 54, 72, 83–5, 102, 105, 141, 158, 159, 164, 193
rational planning 14–5, 62–6, 71
rationality 32, 62–82
realism 108–12
reflection 149–56
reflexiveness 149–56
regional difference 145
relativism 96, 107
reliability 21
research 20–3, 38–40, 47, 48–9, 97, 123, 131
research methods 8, 23, 93, 137–8, 142, 146
research-minded 21, 75
residential 12, 28, 31–5, 37–8, 38–40, 90–1, 111, 124, 140, 180
revenue 13
reviews 57
rights 33, 60, 72, 116, 126, 142, 174–81, 184

scientific method 37–8, 45, 46–9, 51–3, 85, 105, 114, 140
serial evaluation 132
sex and sexism 23, 24, 104
sexual abuse 31
sexual harassment 116
sexual orientation 11, 17, 20, 26, 98, 99, 100, 103, 114, 159, 161, 164, 193
silencing 32, 146
staff teams 30, 38–40, 53, 111, 128–30
stakeholder evaluation 86, 89–92, 92–5, 100–1, 121, 135–6, 159–60
statistics 27, 63, 69–70, 76–8, 81
street-level bureaucrat 44, 64
social class 11, 17, 20, 26, 32, 98, 99, 100, 104, 111, 114, 159, 160, 161, 164, 193
social construction 48, 86–7, 94, 106
social control 25–7, 41, 62–6, 73, 159
social engineering 44
social exclusion 152–3
social experiment 42
social need 16, 71, 79, 115
social security 124–6
social services department 15, 28, 38–40, 58–9, 60–2, 74–5, 90–1, 119–22, 128–30
Social Services Inspectorate 16, 121, 126, 136

socio-economic factors 10, 17, 20, 145
sources of data 23, 147
subjectivity 5, 7, 11, 12, 84, 86–8, 89, 93, 98, 100, 102, 105–6, 108, 112–13, 149, 159–62
summative evaluation 88
supervision 154–6

talk 26, 28–9, 33, 55, 112–18, 127–8, 139, 144, 147–9, 161–2, 179–81
targets 74, 76–9, 125, 128–30
task-centred work 10
Taylorism 45
texts 106, 131, 149–54, 161–2, 178–81
think-tanks 14–15
throughputs 11, 61, 79
training 22, 38, 119
triangulation 148
truths 48, 49, 50, 52, 100, 104–6, 112, 151–2, 158–62, 163, 170–6, 188

unemployment 13, 27
user participation 14, 15, 55, 71, 138–45, 154
user surveys 57, 76, 80, 86, 137–8, 138–45, 147, 150
users 6, 12, 17, 22, 24, 26, 41, 54, 69, 71–3, 76, 87, 103, 127–8, 162, 177
utilisation 44–5, 89–90

validity 21
value for money 1, 14, 25, 57, 60, 126
values 6, 23–5, 31–5, 48–9, 57, 59, 60, 62, 75, 84, 86–7, 89, 99, 102, 117–18, 162, 169–74, 177, 192–3, 189, 194
voluntary projects 22, 27, 28, 37–8, 100–1, 138, 143

welfare pluralism 14, 123
Welfare State 13–18, 123, 182, 183–6, 188–90
women's education 152–3

young people 38–40, 71, 100–1, 117, 143